Katrin Erdmann

SO HELP ME GOD

Katrin Erdmann

SO HELP ME GOD
The Influence of the Religious Right
on the Campaigning of George W. Bush

LIT

Bibliographic information published by Die Deutsche Bibliothek
Die Deutsche Bibliothek lists this publication in the Deutsche
Nationalbibliografie; detailed bibliographic data are available in the
Internet at http://dnb.ddb.de.

ISBN 3-8258-9467-3
Zugl.: Hannover, Univ., Diss., 2004

A catalogue record for this book is available from the British Library

© LIT VERLAG Hamburg 2006
Auslieferung/Verlagskontakt:
Grevener Str./Fresnostr. 2 48159 Münster
Tel. +49 (0)251–62 03 20 Fax +49 (0)251–23 19 72
e-Mail: lit@lit-verlag.de http://www.lit-verlag.de

Distributed in the UK by: Global Book Marketing, 99B Wallis Rd, London, E9 5LN
Phone: +44 (0) 20 8533 5800 – Fax: +44 (0) 1600 775 663
http://www.centralbooks.co.uk/acatalog/search.html

Distributed in North America by:

Transaction Publishers
New Brunswick (U.S.A.) and London (U.K.)

Transaction Publishers
Rutgers University
35 Berrue Circle
Piscataway, NJ 08854

Phone: +1 (732) 445 - 2280
Fax: + 1 (732) 445 - 3138
for orders (U. S. only):
toll free (888) 999 - 6778
e-mail:
orders@transactionspub.com

For my parents

Heike Brinkmann
& Walter Erdmann

and for

Amie Radenbaugh

Acknowledgements

This book would not have been possible without a number of people. Prof. Dr. Christiane Lemke who guided me through the process in a very unbureaucratic and helpful way. Amie Radenbaugh who from beginning to end was there with inspiration, motivation, and everything else. Uwe Prions whose uncomplicated IT expertise and advice made everything much easier.

I would also like to thank the IMPRESS Boston team, especially Marc Elmhorst, Carsten Muenx, Rich Hamlin, Martin Stenzig and Malcolm van Hilten. Furthermore Kirsten Schlingmann, Dr. Stephan Meyer, Fahim Alefi, Sally van Hilten, Jennie Record, Tamara and Holger Blume, Carsten Remmert, Daniel Kunze, Elke Neumann and Martin Cullen for understanding and advice never unsolicited. Wilhelm and Lucie Brinkmann for encouragement, intellectual stimulation and many, many questions & answers.

Last but not least I would like to thank my parents, Heike Brinkmann and Walter Erdmann for the years of support.

Christiane Lemke

Vorwort

Die Vereinigten Staaten sind ein durch Religion nachhaltig geprägtes Land. Nicht erst seit den Terroranschlägen vom 11. September 2001 sind religiöse Werte und Symbole von prägender Bedeutung für die Politik. Vielmehr gehören religiöse Überzeugungen und Deutungsmuster zur Gründungserfahrung der Vereinigten Staaten, und sie sind tief im Alltag verankert. Historisch bildeten religiöse Unterdrückung und Verfolgung, Marginalisierung und Ausgrenzung in der „alten Welt" ein treibendes Motiv zur Auswanderung und Ansiedlung immer neuer Generationen von Einwanderern. Mit der „neuen Welt" waren stets Hoffnungen auf ein besseres Leben verknüpft, und die Freiheit der Religionsausübung, wie auch die Vorstellung von der guten Gesellschaft begründeten die spezifisch amerikanische Form der Zivilreligion, in der Alltag und religiöse Überzeugungen untrennbar miteinander verwoben sind. Aus dieser Erfahrung ergibt sich der zentrale Platz, den Religion im Gründungsmythos der Vereinigten Staaten und in der Identitätsbildung der Gesellschaft einnimmt.

Auch heute noch sind religiöse Werte und Vorstellungen weit in der amerikanischen Gesellschaft verbreitet. Während in den Ländern Europas religiöse Bindungen und religiöser Glauben stetig an Bedeutung verloren haben und mit Ausnahme einiger weniger Länder in der politischen Identität kaum eine Rolle spielen, gilt für die USA eine gegensätzliche Entwicklung. Religion ist unverändert ein wichtiger Faktor des persönlichen und gesellschaftlichen Lebens, und sie beeinflusst die amerikanische Gesellschaft in vielfacher Hinsicht. So hat sich beispielsweise die Kirchgangshäufigkeit in den letzten fünfzig Jahren so gut wie nicht verändert; etwa Dreiviertel der Amerikanerinnen und Amerikaner sind Mitglied einer Kirche oder kirchlichen Gemeinschaft und mehr als die Hälfte geben an, dass Religion sehr bedeutsam und immerhin noch ein Drittel, dass Religion bedeutsam für ihr privates Leben sei, im Vergleich zu Europäern, von denen durchschnittlich weniger als die Hälfte die Religion für ihr eigenes Leben als bedeutsam einschätzen.

Bereits Max Weber erkannte zu Beginn des 20. Jahrhunderts die herausragende Rolle religiöser Einstellungen und Organisationsformen in der amerikanischen Gesellschaft. Die rasante Entwicklung des Kapitalismus in den USA beruhte nach Weber nicht zuletzt auf dem puritanischen Erbe, aufgrund dessen sich selbst der „moderne Mensch", so Weber, offen zu seiner Religiosität bekannte. Die beiden großen politischen Parteien haben sich historisch allerdings weitgehend von religiösen Festlegungen ferngehalten, um so als Sammelbecken sehr unterschiedlicher weltanschaulicher und gesellschaftlicher Strömungen fungieren zu können. Wie Studien zeigen, ist es für die amerikanische Gesellschaft charakteristisch, dass Religiosität für sich genommen noch kein Kriterium für ein distinktes politisches Verhalten ist. Der Glaube an Gott und die starke religiöse Bindung an die Glaubensgemeinschaft im Alltagsleben sind beispielsweise unter schwarzen Baptisten, konservativen Evangelikalen und hispanischer katholischer Bevölkerung nahezu gleichermaßen stark, aber sie ziehen aufgrund ihrer unterschiedlichen historischen und politisch-kulturellen Erfahrungen verschiedene politische Folgerungen. Strenggläubige Protestanten fühlen sich eher der Republikanischen Partei verbunden, Afroamerikaner und, mehrheitlich, auch die hispanische Bevölkerung aber den Demokraten.

Religiöser Pluralismus mit einer inzwischen unübersehbaren Zahl unterschiedlicher religiöser Glaubensrichtungen charakterisiert die heutige amerikanische Realität. Angesichts der gesellschaftlichen Schlüsselstellung von Religion überrascht es nicht, dass religiöse Orientierungen in politischen Auseinandersetzungen und in Wahlkämpfen eine wichtige Rolle spielen. Die Politisierung von christlich-fundamentalistischen Gruppen und ihr stetig wachsender Einfluss auf die US-amerikanische Regierung ist jedoch ein relativ neues Phänomen des ausgehenden 20. Jahrhunderts. Amerikanische Präsidenten haben zwar in der Regel ihre Legitimation auch aus zivilreligiösen Überzeugungen hergeleitet, aber sie haben es historisch weitgehend vermieden, einer religiösen Gruppierung besonderen Zugang zur Macht zu gewähren.

Der politische Aufstieg des christlich-protestantischen Fundamentalismus setzt bereits in den achtziger Jahren, mit der Präsidentschaft von Ronald Reagan, ein. Im Jahr 2000 trat die religiöse Rechte dann als Wählerblock für die republikanische Partei auf, und sie hat in den vergangenen Jahren weiter an Einfluss gewinnen können. Mit der Wahl von George W. Bush hat schließlich ein Präsident Einzug in das Weiße Haus gehalten, der seine Legitimation immer wieder direkt auf Gott bezieht und der seine Machtposition nicht zuletzt einer gezielten und effektiven Mobilisierung im christlich-fundamentalistischen Feld verdankt. In Sprache, Metaphern und Rhetorik verleiht er seinen religiös fundierten Auffassungen Ausdruck und sucht christlich-moralische Autorität in einer Zeit rasanten gesellschaftlichen und globalen Wandels zu verkörpern. Es ist diese religiöse Selbstinszenierung, mit der der Präsident seinen Machtanspruch untermauert, die in Europa und anderen Teilen der Welt immer wieder Befremden und Ablehnung auslöst.

Mit der vorliegenden Studie zeigt Katrin Erdmann anhand der Präsidentschaftswahlen im Jahr 2000, wie es der religiösen Rechten gelang, im Wahlkampf einen entscheidenden Einfluss auszuüben und George W. Bush zur Macht zu verhelfen. Die Autorin begreift die religiöse Rechte als soziale Bewegung, die zunächst außerhalb politischer Institutionen in der breiteren Gesellschaft entstanden ist, und schließlich nach der politischen Macht griff, um ihr Ziel einer gläubigen, christlichen Gesellschaft umzusetzen. Entscheidend für den Aufstieg von einer Basisbewegung zu einer politischen Kraft waren die Öffnung zum konservativen *Mainstream* und zu den Neokonservativen, die nicht zuletzt über persönliche Verbindungen und Netzwerke zustande kam, sowie schließlich die Transformation in eine Wahlallianz für die republikanische Partei. Präzise beschreibt die Autorin das politische Umfeld, in welchem die heterogen strukturierten christlich-fundamentalistischen Bewegungen agieren, die Bildung von basisnahen Organisationen sowie die wechselseitigen, auch personell begründeten Arbeitsbeziehungen zwischen Neokonservativen und religiösen Gruppen, die dem christlichen Fundamentalismus zum Aufstieg verholfen haben.

Den Kern der religiösen Rechten bilden die christlich-fundamentalistischen Evangelikalen, die in einer Vielzahl von Kirchengemeinden und Vereinigungen organisiert sind, und die inzwischen über ein weit verzweigtes Netz von *think tanks* und öffentlichen Meinungsgebern für gesellschafts- und außenpolitische Themen verfügen. Durch Professionalisierung und den Einsatz neuer Medien gewann die Bewegung an Einfluss, neue Gruppierungen setzten sich durch, und zwar nicht nur im traditionell religiösen *bible belt* der Südstaaten, sondern auch im Westen und Mittleren Westen der USA. Abgestützt durch eine Parallelgesellschaft, mit - teilweise kommerziell erfolgreich agierenden – alltagsweltlich verzweigten Gemeindestrukturen und „Megakirchen" und unterstützt durch eine religiöse Mobilisierung, wird eine politische Polarisierung vorangetrieben, die dem republikanischen Feld einen deutlichen Stimmenzuwachs beschert hat.

Wie Katrin Erdmann zeigt, bleiben die Organisationsstrukturen der religiösen Rechten dezentral und fragmentiert, aber moralische Themen mit hoher lebensweltlicher Relevanz, die die religiöse Rechte aufgreift - wie Ehe- und Familienwerte, Homosexualität, Abtreibung sowie Fragen von Krankheit, Sterben und Tod - ergeben ein großes Mobilisationspotential, auf das gerade in Wahlkämpfen zurückgegriffen werden kann. Die Einwerbung von Wahlkampfspenden, Öffentlichkeitsarbeit sowie personalpolitische Entscheidungen nehmen einen zentralen Platz in der Arbeit der Basisgruppen ein. So kann die Verfasserin zeigen, dass sich führende Vertreter der religiösen Rechten bereits frühzeitig auf G. W. Bush als Präsidentschaftskandidaten festgelegt und andere Kandidaten der Republikaner gezielt diskreditiert hatten. Bereits in den Vorwahlen konnte die religiöse Rechte so Weichen stellen, selbst in Bundesstaaten mit einer mehrheitlich nicht-protestantischen Wählerschaft. Trotz der verfassungsrechtlichen Trennung von Kirche und Staat üben die christlich-fundamentalistischen Gruppen daher einen größeren und direkteren Einfluss auf die Politik der amerikanischen Regierung aus, als in der Vergangenheit.

Die vorliegende Forschungsarbeit, die als Dissertation an der Universität Hannover entstanden ist und auf umfangreichen Bibliotheks- und Feldstudien in den USA beruht, liefert einen äußerst wichtigen Beitrag zur Analyse der amerikanischen Gesellschaft, da sie ein zentrales Feld der politischen Soziologie amerikanischer Parteien und sozialer Bewegungen beleuchtet. Mit ihrer fundierten Analyse und präzisen Darstellung trägt die Autorin zum Verständnis einer hochbrisanten Entwicklung der US-amerikanischen Gesellschaft bei, die heute an Aktualität kaum zu übertreffen ist.

Die religiöse Rechte bestimmt auch in der zweiten Amtszeit von George W. Bush weitgehend die gesellschaftspolitische Agenda der Republikaner. Allerdings bleiben die Radikalisierung der religiösen Rechten und ihr wachsender politischer Einfluss in den Vereinigten Staaten nicht unwidersprochen. Führende Republikaner insistieren, dass es der Tradition der Partei entspricht, mehr zu repräsentieren, als die christliche Rechte vorgibt. Die religiös-fundamentalistische Festlegung in gesellschaftlichen Grundfragen stößt vor allem bei liberalen und moderaten Republikanern auf Widerspruch, die darauf beharren, dass die Geschichte der Partei vornehmlich von den Ideen der Selbstbestimmung und der individuellen Freiheitsrechte geprägt sei.

Auch vielen traditionellen Glaubensgemeinschaften geht die Politisierung zu weit, denn die religiösen Gemeinschaften haben ihr Aktionsfeld vor allem im kommunalen und nachbarschaftlichen Bereich, und nicht in der Bundespolitik entfaltet. Machtpolitische Ansprüche sind dem Konzept der Zivilreligion eher fremd. So sind die Grenzen fundamentalistischer Mobilisierung vermutlich bereits erreicht, zumal das Gesellschaftsmodell der religiösen Gruppen relativ homogenen sozialen Einheiten auf der Ebene von Gemeinden entlehnt und für pluralistische, hochkomplexe

Gesellschaften mittelfristig wenig tauglich ist. Die gesellschaftlichen Bruchlinien sind bereits sichtbar, aber es ist bislang weder der moderaten Mitte noch den Liberalen gelungen, die Deutungsmacht über moralische Fragen wiederzuerlangen und eine politische Gegenmacht abzustützen. Derweil bleibt die amerikanische Bevölkerung in ihren Überzeugungen weiter gespalten.

Hannover, im August 2005

Table of Contents

0. Introduction   1

    0.1. Problem and Goal   1
    0.2. Structure   2

1. The Religious Right and Neo-conservatism in the U.S.A   4

    1.1. The Religious Right as a Social Movement   4

       1.1.1. The Social Movement of the Religious Right   5
       1.1.2. Strategy and Ideology of the Movement   7
       1.1.3. The Movement's Strengths   11
       1.1.4. Case Study: A Christian Fundamentalist Mother and Her Lifestyle   16

          1.1.4.1. Personality   16
          1.1.4.2. Background   16
          1.1.4.3. Family   17
          1.1.4.4. Religious Life   17
          1.1.4.5. Home Schooling   17
          1.1.4.6. General Life   18

1.2. The Religious Right and Neo-conservatism 19

    1.2.1. Neo-conservatism and the New Right 19
    1.2.2. Ideology 26
    1.2.3. The Religious Right and Education 28
    1.2.4. The Religious Right and Governmental Involvement 29
    1.2.5. Democratic Values 30
    1.2.6. International Politics 31
    1.2.7. Shared Values of the New Right and Neo-conservatives 34

1.3. Aspects of the History of the Religious Right 38

    1.3.1. Early Beginnings 38
    1.3.2. Fundamentalism 40
    1.3.3. The Third Wave 44
    1.3.4. The Robertson Candidacy 46
    1.3.5. The Religious Right in the 1990's 49

2. Structures and Political Influence of the Religious Right 52

2.1. Organizations of the Religious Right 52

2.2. Organizational Structures of the Religious Right 56
    2.2.1. The Christian Coalition 56
    2.2.2. Focus On the Family 61
    2.2.3. The National Right to Life Committee 65

2.2.4. Concerned Women for America	67
2.2.5. The Promise Keepers	71
2.3. Leaders of the Religious Right	77
2.3.1. Marion "Pat" Robertson	77
2.3.2. Ralph Reed	88
2.3.3. James C. Dobson	90

3. The Campaign   93

3.1. Channels and Mechanisms of Influence	93
3.1.1. Connecting Congregations to Political Processes	93
3.1.2. Faith and Politics	96
3.1.3. Clerical Encouragement	97
3.1.4. Community Outreach	98
3.1.5. White Evangelical Churches	102
3.2. Aspects of the Financing of the 2000 Campaign	103
3.2.1. The Bush Approach	103
3.2.2. The Primaries	105
3.2.3. The Presidential General Election	111
3.3. Media and the 2000 Election	114
3.3.1. Religious Right Usage of the Media	114
3.3.2. Media Distribution via Think Tanks	116
3.3.3. Bush, Gore and the Media	118

3.4. Which Candidates Were of Interest to the Religious Right	121
3.4.1. Leading up to the Primaries	121
3.4.2. The Primary in New Hampshire	123
3.4.3. The South Carolina Primary	124
3.4.4. Michigan	125
3.4.5. Virginia	126
3.4.6. Conclusion	128
3.5. The Image George W. Bush Draws of Himself	129
3.5.1. Bush Presenting Himself in Front of the Media	129
3.5.2. Bush in Speeches	132
3.5.2.1. Videotaped Remarks to the Christian Coalition Road to Victory	134
3.5.2.2. Speech: A New Prosperity: Seats for All at the Welcome Table	137
3.5.3. Conclusion	139
4. Conclusion	**141**
5. Bibliography	**145**
6. Appendix	**162**

0. Introduction

0.1. Problem and Goal

Religion and politics have always had a close relationship in United States policy making despite the constitutional guarantee of the separation of Church and State. The Pilgrims[1], coming to the New World in order to escape prosecution for religious beliefs, shaped the young country's value system in ways that are still prevalent to this day.

> "Most Americans today, of course, are no longer Puritan in morals, but Puritan ways of thinking about work, the family, and society still influence America at the beginning of the third millennium. Calvin's theology has not endured--the doctrine of predestination, for example, has long since been abandoned by most Protestant Americans--but his social and cultural views still resonate" (Doyle 2000: 38).

The discussion about the separation of Church and State are just one indicator for the outstanding position that the "faith factor" (Adams 1998) has in the United States. Many U.S. citizens see their country as a Christian nation, as God's own country where battles have to be fought between "good" and "evil".

There are numerous examples of this influence: from the former faith in predestination theory[2] which had a large impact on much of the economic

---

[1] For further reading see: "Why America is different: Puritans, circuit riders, and the free market". Contributors: Rodger Doyle – author. In *Free Inquiry*. Volume: 22. Issue: 3. Publication Date: Summer 2002.

[2] Predestination theory states that a person is already chosen or not chosen to go to heaven while still living on earth. People can try to look for signs which indicate whether they are chosen or not; one of the signs is whether one is successful in monetary terms or not. This is in direct contradiction to Matthew 19:24 where it says: "Again I tell you, it is easier for a camel to go through the eye of a needle than for a rich man to enter the kingdom of God." A clear example on how a handful of people have interpreted the Bible in a way that later on became a whole belief system DESPITE its clash with Scripture. Modern theology will interpret this part by stating that the term "ear of a needle" was also used in order to describe the small gates into the cities during biblical times. A camel would have to be unloaded in order to fit through the gate. This makes it DIFFICULT for a rich person to enter heaven, but, unlike the literal interpretation of the Bible, not IMPOSSIBLE. Many of the Religious Right leaders are fairly rich due to their activities which they commonly do not disclose to their audience.

beliefs to the fact that the overwhelming majority of American presidents have belonged to a protestant denomination.

While this influence has always been there, mainly in an underlying way, (for example, no president would be elected without acknowledging their belief in God and their regular church attendance.), in the past 25 years, its influence has become much more dominant. Starting with former Democratic President Jimmy Carter, the previously apolitical evangelical movement has been recruited to become active in the political sphere. It is a growing movement that had its latest success in the election of a President that heads a country with military spending higher than the next 10 countries on the list. He is a President who says of himself that he is deeply religious and a born-again Christian, who gives speeches oozing with biblical references and who emphasizes Judeo-Christian values at every possible occasion.

In this paper I will try to analyze a possiple influence of the Religious Right on the campaigning of George W. Bush in the 2000 election. I will focus on the question whether the Religious Right was a decisive factor for the outcome of the of the election. The theoretic approach will be based on the discussion about social movements in the USA and how the Religious Right constitutes as a social movement.

0.2. Structure

The first Chapter will describe how American Evangelicals became associated with the Republican Party and how they were utilized as they were merged with the neo-conservative movement. Furthermore, it describes how the resulting social movement has evolved from this merger and has been very successful at grass-roots lobbying. In addition, the first Chapter will give a brief overview of the history of the Religious Right, concentrating on the years from 1980 to the mid 1990's, since these were crucial to the shaping of the movement. Often enough the Religious Right is being seen as the heart of a strong evangelical movement with homogenous political goals and issues. With the help of a matrix, I will describe different organizations and thus demonstrate the heterogenous nature of the movement.

The second Chapter will describe different aspects of the Religious Right. From an overview of different groups, to a more in depth analysis of some of the most important organizations, as well as their head figures, it will try to show some of the underlying structures.

In the third Chapter, I will take a closer look at the campaign itself, trying to determine which role the media plays. Furthermore, I will look at the candidates that received attention from the Religious Right and which states proved to be of importance. The channels of influence that exist for religion to influence voters are further discussed in this chapter. In the past, the earlier success of the Christian Coalition in the primaries has not led to success in the actual elections. The picking of a few issues however enables the Religious Right to focus its strength onto certain areas. I will examine how the influence of the leaders of the Religious Right has an effect on the campaigning itself. Furthermore I will look at how candidates and in particular George W. Bush cater their campaigning at the Religious Right.

As the actions of this administration are unfolding, it becomes more and more clear, how an important factor a faction is that can make a certain person President. The policy changes that have been introduced since after September 11th reflect the views of an individual that has been appointed for office as a thank you to the Religious Right: John Ashcroft. His policies, as well as those of the Secretary of Defense Donald Rumsfeld, are what have been shaping this Bush administration the most. Both fit neatly into the package that the Religious Right wanted to see in office for their own purposes. Bush knew about the voting potential of Christian Conservatives, whom he courted throughout the entire campaign.

In my paper, I will show the link between the so called Religious Right and the Bush 2000 presidential election campaign. I will try to determine how much of an impact the Religious Right had on the outcome of this election, especially considering that it was such a close election. While Bush lost the popular vote, he won the electoral vote, which in part could mean that the Religious Right made a difference where it was important.

1. The Religious Right and Neo-conservatism in the U.S.A

1.1. The Religious Right as a Social Movement

Collective action in the U.S. exists in such a magnitude that its complexity partly adds to the ambiguity that is surrounding definitions of what a social movement is. According to Williams (2000: 51), a general definition of a social movement incorporates "organized groups that act consciously and with some continuity to promote or resist change through collective action". This collective action is sustained and organized in some form. However, there is a difference between a social movement and a social movement organization. Among others, Guigni has pointed out the relevance of distinguishing between the different types of collective action and systematically identifying actions emerging from social movement organizations and mobilization (1998: xiii).

Charles Tilly states that the characteristics of a social movement include "sustained challenge to power holders in the name of a population living under the jurisdiction of those power holders by means of repeated public displays of that population's numbers, commitment, unity, and worthiness" (Guigni, McAdam and Tilly 1998: 7). This definition vaguely implies a structural or institutional component to social movements. However, a clearer definition of the role of organization structure and movement resources in the mobilization of social movements can be found in McCarthy and Zald (1977), McAdam and Snow (1997), and Tarrow (1998).

According to Tarrow, a contentious political issue such as abortion or family values can mobilize groups that are "backed by dense social networks and galvanized by culturally resonant, action-oriented symbols" and thus accumulate in "sustained interaction with opponents" (1998: 2). Pre-existing social networks are playing an important part in facilitating the emergence of social movements in his theory, but actual *social movement organizations* as mentioned by McCarthy and Zald (1977) are being omitted.

Turner and Killian (1965: 308) argue that "a social movement is a collectivity acting with some continuity to promote or resist a change in the society or group of which it is a part" not differentiating between, as Freeman (1999) calls it, "movement as organization" and "movement as a community of like minded adherents or supporters of larger organizational goals and agendas".

McAdams' (1997) definition of social movements is more systematic and detailed: "A collectivity acting with some degree of organization and continuity outside of institutional channels for the purpose of promoting or resisting change in the group, society, or world order of which it is a part" (xviii). However, this definition seems to imply that movements act exclusively outside the institutional channel rather than transforming institutions from the inside. While social movements have to be distinguished from political groups such as lobbying associations, studies on the civil rights and women's rights movements and their relationship to the Democratic party (Freeman, 1999; Baer and Bositis, 1993) provide evidence that it is indeed possible for a social movement to act inside an institutional channel.

In order to have an impact on a state's policy, the influence from inside concurs with the political process theory of social movements as McFarland (1998: 12) states: "Movement leaders have defined a social problem, have linked it with proposed social solutions, and are looking for an opportunity to get the state to implement their proposed policies". The sustained collective action is what also distinguishes social movements from ephemeral groups. In my paper, I will adhere to the Turner and Kilian definition of a social movement.

1.1.1. The Social Movement of the Religious Right

The status of social movement organizations is closely linked to their organization being outside the institutional channels, because it supports their role of extra-state actors. The members of these social movement organizations are very capable of integrating into and influencing political institutions, e.g. as voters, activists or candidates. The Christian Coalition can be referred to as a social movement organization which will stay outside the institutional channels. The label "Religious Right" however, is a name for a community of like minded individuals, who are very likely to act from within *and* outside of political institutional channels.

The Religious Right social movement in particular consists primarily of theologically motivated Christian reactionaries. These reactionaries are usually working within the electoral system and are trying to impose their religious views on morality and culture as binding for secular society. It is a right-wing movement which is in particular working to promote moral traditionalism and which sees the state as an enforcer rather than a distributor (Diamond 1995: 9).

Several American social movement organizations have been rooted in beliefs and values that were based on religious faith. The 19th-century American Protective Association and Anti-Saloon League as well as the more current organizations such as the Christian Coalition, Operation Rescue or the Promise Keepers belong to these organizations. Tactics have changed since the beginning of social movements in ante bellum America, when among other issues, activists were primarily concerned with slavery, alcohol, and Catholics. The issues were usually picked up by the major parties which continued to happen into the 20th century. Much of it was absorbed into the "consolidating institutional structure of the parties" (Williams 1998: 53) and from there into the federal government.

In the 20th century, political issues became less local. This was partly due to a new social mobility and to increased information technology. Politics were dominated by the two major parties, each relying on a solid constituency base.

This has changed over the past half century with "anti-party" campaign platforms being more popular than ever, and due to the fact that being a member of the Washington Beltway has a negative connotation to it for many Americans[5]. More and more Americans consider themselves as independent rather than belonging to the constituency of one of the two major parties. As Williams (1998: 53) states "[A]lthough parties still matter enormously in the institutional workings of established government, they have lost their place as the culturally approved way of organizing political attitudes and loyalties". Washington D.C. is today's center of action. More and more social movements have their activities taking place in the nation's capital, and politics has become increasingly national. The 1997 Promise Keeper's rally on Washington, although claimed to have no political aim, took place in the nation's capital in order to nationalize the movement.

The Religious Right as a social movement is aiming at the restoration of "traditional values" in public policy through the mobilization of evangelical Protestants and other conservative religious communities for political action. Challenging political institutions in order to redress its grievances is a

---

[5] Recent scandals involving members of the federal government such as the Clinton/Lewinsky, Chandra Levy/Senator Gary Condit or, most recently, the Enron case have not helped to improve Washington's reputation.

fundamental part of this restoration, which is similar to other social movements. The Religious Right has focused this challenge mainly at the ballot box, paying special attention to the Republican Party (Oldfield 1996). However political parties represent heterogeneous groups and issues[6], in order to gather as many votes as possible. As single-issue politics is anathema for political parties, compromises are made, and some of those compromises upset other factions of the party. Social movements can pursue a single cause with dedicated adherents that are often passionate and morally committed to the issue. This often makes social movements more vibrant than parties but also more fragile, because these passions about a single issue (e.g. Abortion) or a narrow set of issues (e.g. Family values) have to be kept alive in order to keep the adherents involved.

In order to secure the support of the adherents, social movements first of all need to call attention to an actual or exaggerated injustice. This injustice, in the eye of the activist, requires action in order to be removed. Secondly, an identity has to be established. This enables the adherents to distinguish between "friend" and "enemy on a factual and, even more importantly, on an emotional level. The change that is anticipated must seem achievable. Public movement rhetoric seems very radical;, however, taking the preceding factors into consideration, this radicalization comes as no surprise[7]. In order to achieve a level of involvement by the adherents that will make them dedicate time and money outside their normal lives to a common goal and a group ideology and for the media to pay attention to a certain social movement and its ideology, radicalization is a common strategy.

1.1.2. Strategy and Ideology of the Movement

Soper (1992) states that group ideology plays a major role in understanding the emergence and political strategies as well as the timing of social

---

[6] One example in George W. Bush's campaign was his meeting with the leader of the gay Republicans organization and in order to demonstrate his open-mindedness for their cause. On the other hand, while his appointment of John Ashcroft, who has very close links to the Religious Right, was a slap in the face for the gay activists in the Republican party. However, the inauguration ceremony was attended by Vice President Richard Cheney's openly lesbian daughter and her partner which presented a novelty.

[7] For an example on movement rhetoric see Williams (2000)

movements in opposition to other theories which rely more on state structure, rational choice,

resource mobilization, grievance theories or group status. He gives the examples of the anti-abortion and the temperance movements to show the impact that group ideology has on the formation and process these two movements went through.

> "I contend that social movements tend to emerge and take hold when there is a disruption in the moral order which challenges the coherence, norms, or beliefs of an ideology. When social conditions change in such a way as to make the obligations or intelligibility of a belief system inoperable, social movements will arise to reconstruct the coherence or values of the ideology. An ideology provides the beliefs and values which help structure group objectives, the norms of commitment and obligation which lead people to join organizations, and the meaning to legitimate group formation" (1992: 51).

The willingness to contribute large amounts of time and resources as well as substantial financial contributions in combination with very motivated individuals of their movement is a characteristic which is deeply rooted in the history of the Christian conservative movements in the United States.

> "All in all, professional activism, supported by a variety of issues and constituencies and oriented toward a national political scene, has become a major force in U.S. politics in the past 30 years" (Williams 2000: 51).

One of the reasons for becoming a major force in national politics is the somewhat professional approach that some social movement organizations, secular or faith based, take. The social changes of the 1960's had a culture of protest emerge which included networks, organizing techniques and experienced activists. The knowledge acquired by these activists was taken up and put to use by other organizations as well. Newly learned formal organization skills facilitated strategy development as well as communication, fund-raising, recruitment and instrumentalization of the media - especially for organizations that could not rely on pre-existing networks. Since their followers were recruited across social categories and groups instead of out of a pre-existing constituencies, these strategies which had been tested in previous years were an invaluable tactical source.

These professional social movement organizations are not only beneficial for their adherents. Politicians can use them as well, as a clear opposition leader, someone to negotiate with, and as a catalyst for channeling ideological claims. Professional social movement organizations are more costly than lose networks but, at the same time, can act more efficiently. The more staff that is hired in order to be able to compete on the national stage, the more bureaucracy is necessary to rally and secure support from followers and sympathizers. More bureaucracy and more qualified professional activists mean it is more costly to run the organization. Also, if there is more than one social movement organization per social movement, organizations start competing against each other, because their constituents will come from roughly the same pool. Competing against each other will again cost time, money and energy that otherwise could be spent on the main cause.

When more solid structures develop due to professionalization of an organization, the organization most likely becomes less flexible in its strategies and tactics. Looking at Operation Rescue[8] as an example, the organization's tactic of besieging abortion clinics ossified over time and made it possible for its opponents to respond accordingly. When the organization's tactics changed and became much more radical and violent, many adherents were not willing to follow. At the same time, the more violent organizations such as the Lambs of God were not very likely to participate in Operation Rescue's actions (Diamond 1998).

One advantage that faith based social movement organizations have is that their constituency is usually organized already. The congregations themselves can provide newly forming organizations with meeting places, fund-raising capacities and already existing social networks. Furthermore, these networks extend beyond the congregation into the community and sometimes even further. The infrastructure that is needed to building up an organization is already there. The Promise Keepers[9] are just one example of how many followers a movement organization can have by using already established structures. Also, religious congregations usually have a constituency which can be considered fairly homogeneous. Since belonging

---

[8] Operation Rescue (OR) was founded in 1987 by Joseph Scheidler. Its aim was to actively hinder women from receiving abortions at abortion clinics. Starting out, activists besieged clinics and physically blocked the entrances to abortion facilities. As the organization grew, it became more militant. Members of OR have been conviceted of bombing abortion clinics and even murdering doctors that have performed abortions (Diamond 1998).
[9] For more information on the Promise Keepers see chapter 2.2.5.

to a certain church or denomination is decided upon by the individual or their family, these denominations are usually local, and their members often differ from other denominations by race, ethnicity, economic class and locality. Thus, one congregation usually gives access to a greater body of likeminded and networking people who are already used to cooperating.

Regardless of how important of a part the congregations have in forming social movement organizations, they rarely become such an organization themselves. The multi purpose functions that churches have in a community include more than this aspect. Churches serve spiritual, social and practical needs and by turning into a social movement organization, they risk losing that part of their congregation that does not believe in taking political action or does not agree with the particular direction a movement is going. Also, the church's tax exemption status could be at risk by displaying any political activity.

The spiritual leaders of a congregation usually tend to tolerate, rather than to lead, activities that go in the direction of social movements. Too much involvement could again lead parts of the congregation to leave a certain church, and especially the so called "free churches", churches that employ a congregational policy rather than belonging to an institution, are vulnerable to losing members as they provide the salary of the clergy.

The rhetoric of religion is often an important factor in recruiting new members. Religious symbolism and the language of "good" and "evil" are instruments showing that there is more to a cause than just materialistic interests. This type of language is easily understood by a vast majority of people as religion has a firm place in every day life of many Americans. However, different audiences must receive language "custom tailored" to their needs. While a more sectarian approach will convince the faithful and can turn them into fervent constituents by, for example, distinguishing "them from "us, an approach with a nonsectarian, civil religious language with an ecumenical taste to it that maximizes similarities and embraces many will more likely convince elected officials and persuade bystanders.

This fine balance is difficult to keep. Earlier statements by members of the Moral Majority made about how God does not hear the prayers of Jews (Williams 1998: 60) gave the Moral Majority a reputation of being intolerant which is something they could never quite shake off and which hurt them nationally. On the other hand, Ralph Reed, former director of the Christian Coalition who tried to win votes for the Republican Party, had to leave his position, because he was trying to include a larger number of people by talking about "people of faith" rather than mentioning certain denominations. Many fervent adherents disagreed with such inclusive language.

Biblical texts are the common ground for the shared faith and its political implications; however, this faith can reach further than any direct connection to scripture. Traditional perspectives on sexuality, gender roles and family values (Conover and Gray 1983) play an essential role in the attitudes and beliefs displayed by the movement's adherents.

A political agenda, backed by an ideologically based social movement supported by Christian conservatives, can be linked to the moral reform movements of the 1830's, the temperance movement of the late 19th and early 20th centuries, and to the anti-feminist and anti-suffrage movements of the early 1900's. As it is the concern for the perceived social and moral decline of America that is at the root of many politically active Christian conservatives (Moreland, Steel, and Baker, 1988), the emphasis that the Republican Party has put on "the importance of symbolic conservative values, including the preservation of traditional family values, the importance of religion, support for capital punishment, and opposition to gun control" (Black and Black, 1992: 9) has led to the wide support by Christian conservatives, particularly protestant Christians (Green 2000).

1.1.3. The Movement's Strengths

The vitality of evangelical Protestantism (Jorstad 1993) is one of the main causes of the movement's strengths. Orthodox Christian beliefs are combined with intense individualism which has built a much decentralized set of religious organizations. Parts of these organizations are numerous small denominations, para-church groups and independent churches. These small component institutions form voluntary alliances which make up the bigger groups such as the Southern Baptist Convention. Aggressive, entrepreneurial leaders within these organizations are working to recognize discontent among people, with a special focus on people who *are* already religious. Opportunities are being sought out in order to respond to the discontent and to bring the people together. Organizing the resources to connect people with opportunities is another major job of the organization's leaders.

In a political environment, these leadership skills also come in handy, and as evangelicals have been facing social and economic forces that have made them see lifestyles and views that they, to say the least, strongly disagree with, discontent has grown and brought many opportunities for leaders to use this discontent in order to secure their support. In the views of the evangelical world, these rival values have been protected and even been extended by government policies.

Especially where topics such as abortion, women's roles, family arrangements, the legal status of religion itself, crime and education are concerned, it has been easy for the leaders of this social movement to recruit eager activists that, on the one hand, provide the resources for movement organizations and, on the other hand, are willing to be politically active (Leege 1993: 53). Similar to other politically active Americans, these groups consists mainly of middle class people who have the resources and personal skills to be successful in political activism (Guth in Green 1996: 36). Churches are usually not a formal part of the movement; however, their communities and communication networks are crucial in the recruitment and training of the activists.

The cohesiveness and relative size of evangelicalism in the mass public is another one of the movement's strengths. On a national basis, white evangelicals make up about one fourth of the adult American population, while in the southern and midwestern states, this percentage increases. The very high degree of religious commitment that is present in this percentage of the population is very helpful in terms of mobilization through moral appeals, church communities and religious networks. This group is larger in number than Mainline Protestants or the secular population, and mobilizing just one-half of it would make up a voting bloc that is larger than that of the African Americans, Jews or Episcopalians.

However, the mobilization of this evangelical bloc proves to be rather difficult. The otherworldly orientation of many deeply religious people sometimes accounts for very little interest in politics or even hostility toward it. Also the sometimes different theological beliefs are providing a barrier between the different denominations that is hard to overcome. This extends to the political level where the political concerns may be shared but common action is prohibited by theological differences. This holds true for example for many Catholics and African Americans. Each leader pursues very much their own interest which has not helped cooperation.

Extremists are another problem within the movement. The views expressed by certain members of the Religious Right make them difficult to work with although these very views might have been the incentive to become politically active in the first place. This especially weakens interactions with secular conservatives which are trying to get a broader spectrum behind them and look much more at the pragmatic side of political activities. The mere attempt at trying to broaden the spectrum or compromise on various social issues can become a source of conflict.

The transformation of the evangelical movement to a political movement took place in the late 1970's. Diamond (1995: 165) argues that the emergence of the political movement was due to two factors: policy changes that either had taken place or were proposed and encouragement as well as practical help from the secular New Right. As the secular New Right was concerned with anticommunist militarism, moral traditionalism and economic libertarianism, moral issues rose to the top of the national agenda where the Religious Right set their own emphasis. Since evangelicals constituted a large segment of the population, the secular New Right aimed at instrumentalizing this possible new voting bloc. With the help of the secular New Right, evangelicals formed their own political organizations and joined together to bring Ronald Reagan to the White House (Diamond 1995: 162).

Petchesky (1981) argues that the main focus that brought the secular and religious New Right together were reproductive and sexual issues.

> "If there was anything genuinely 'new' about the current right wing in the United States, it is its tendency to locate sexual, reproductive, and family issues at the center of its political program – not as manipulative rhetoric only, but as the substantive core of a politics geared, on a level that outdistances any previous right-wing movements in this country, to mobilizing a nationwide mass following" (207).

Family and reproductive issues were the issues which evangelicals and many other members of society felt they could actually achieve some influence. The average American had little to say in the fields of economic trends and international relations, and state level politics became a battlefield on which evangelicals could concentrate their focus. According to Diamond (1995: 166) three issues of the 1970's reflected the influence that the counter movement of the New Left had: Legally sanctioned abortions, gay rights initiatives and the Equal Rights Amendment (ERA). All three of these issues dealt with the most personal of relationships and raised questions about traditional roles and relationships between women and men. The nuclear, or as the Religious Right called it, "sacred" family played an important part in this debate, and the role that the state had in order to protect this ideal was highly discussed. These issues were not just a change in the legal code, they were highly symbolic, and in its wake rose questions about curricula, textbooks and school prayer although these were not necessarily related to the counter movement of the New Left.

Remaining consistent with Diamond's definition of right-wing movements wanting the state to play the role of an enforcer of policy rather than being a distributor of power and wealth (Diamond 1995: 9), evangelical activists opposed policies that would distribute power to subordinate groups, in particular women and homosexuals. They expected the state to enforce the traditional roles of women and men and the traditional moral values as well as gender relations. However, when it came to education, these right-wing activists feared nothing more than the "intrusion" of the state into their private lives. These evangelicals saw their ideological and biological prerogatives endangered, just as they saw the prestige of their belief system declining. Their aim was, therefore, to uphold the traditional meaning of the "sacred" family above the one of that the state held.

The secular New Right and the religious New Right did not work against the women's and gay rights movements in an abstract way, but in a practical way by proposing concrete policies on the state and federal level. These exact issues of these 2 movements helped the secular New Right and the religious New Right transform those movements into a working alliance. This was to their mutual advantage since their influence in the political sphere was enhanced by each other and thus grew. Their results in policy making were mixed; however, the public became more aware of this new movement and the early Religious Right became a partisan movement. In the beginning, members of this Religious Right were not the professionals they eventually became in the 1980's and 1990's. Rather, they supported action that was being initiated by right-wing elected officials or other experienced leaders. In the years to come, powerful political organizations would be formed to help the cause of influencing legislation.

The defeat of the Equal Rights Amendment (ERA) and, later on, the fight against civil rights for homosexuals were cases in which members of the religious New Right gained experience, and the movement's level of professionalism grew. However, when the fight against civil rights for homosexuals in the late 1980's intensified, the movement was decentralized and focused locally. The larger organizations of the Religious Right primarily worked in local chapters with ties that were more or less strong to their national headquarter, and different factions were not always pleased with each other.

Judging by the early years, the New Religious Right was a group of people that started to see the world in a similar way, guided by skillful political activists. These activists had strong ties to the secular New Right which they utilized without abandoning their broad constituent's base. For many of these constituents, the perceived decline of traditional order and not the traditional focus on religious matters was the reason they became involved in political action, as opposed to the traditional focus on religious matters.

Their thinking was dominated by the perceived experience of a deep crisis, which is caused by the renunciation of eternally valid, god given and basically inherited principles of structure and morals. They were "real" in a "golden age" once, either in biblical times or in a time about sixty years ago, when the U.S. were perceived as strong and morally intact (Riesebrodt 1990).

1.1.4. Case Study: A Christian Fundamentalist Mother and Her Lifestyle

The following description of a Christian Fundamentalist Mother and Her Lifestyle should be understood to illustrate the lifestyle of somebody close to the movement. It is not meant to be representative for all members of the Religious Right.

Shelly is the mother of four children ranging from the ages of 4 to 11. She has been married for thirteen years and is living with her husband on a dairy farm in Southern Minnesota. The closest village is ca. one mile away and has approximately 14 inhabitants; the closest town of 4,300 inhabitants is about twelve miles away.

1.1.4.1. Personality

She is a very intelligent woman who went to college for a few years before she got married and stopped her education. She is very interested in exercise. She runs several times a week if the weather permits, and during the strong winters in Minnesota, she exercises at home to work-out videos. Accordingly, she is in very good physical shape. She is very sensitive and kind-hearted. Her life revolves around her family and a few church related activities outside of it.

1.1.4.2. Background

Shelly has grown up in a very religious family. Her parents, in particular her mother and grandfather, tried to instill Christian-Judeo values in her and her three siblings. They were all expected to enter marriage as virgins and to lead a life to the glory of God. Her parents are farmers, and Shelly grew up in the rural Minnesotan area where she is now living. Two of her three siblings and her parents live around the same one square mile section that her parents partly own as farm land. Although the rest of her siblings are not nearly as religious as her, there is a strong connection between the siblings. Some of them farm together while others share babysitter responsibilities or exercise with each other.

1.1.4.3. Family

Shelly got married when she was 20 years old to Mark who is a few years older than she is. He finished college with a degree in agriculture. Together, they are running a dairy farm with approximately 80 cows with no outside assistance. The dairy business takes place year-round, while they have time off from the field work during the winter. Clearly, the family is Shelly's central focus point, since there are not any activities that are not somehow related to the family. She is home schooling her children, because she feels that they are not receiving the moral and religious values in a public school that they should receive. She listens to religious broadcasting throughout the day, especially when she is spending time in the car or tractor.

1.1.4.4. Religious Life

Shelly grew up in a Lutheran household that interpreted the bible in literal terms. She believes in a close, personal relationship to God and goes to church every Sunday, if circumstances permit, and during lent, she attends on Wednesdays as well. The country church that her family has belonged to for three generations got a pastor that held a different point of view on baptism than the family and some other members of the congregation. In addition, the Synod they belonged to opened a study group on homosexuality, which in the minds of the family translated into "The synod encourages homosexuality and abortion." After a few months of continuous disagreement, the family left this congregation in order to join a "Free Church" where they have been ever since. The Free Church is much stricter in its interpretations of the bible. Few members have attended college for a full four years. It is clearly the most fundamental church in town.

Shelly's family, however, was discouraged by an inner congregation conflict that resulted in the rejection of a pastor that Shelly liked very much. She and her husband left the congregation and joined a different church in a different town. She teaches Sunday school and sometimes plays the organ.

1.1.4.5. Home Schooling

Shelly follows a curriculum that was designed and published by a religious publisher. Once a week she takes her kids and meets with other home schooling parents at a church basement where they perform simple scientific experiments for the entire group as well as little workshops. They also go swimming at a pool that they rent for a few hours.

1.1.4.6. General Life

The majority of life takes place on the farm or on the farm of her parents. The children are involved in the daily routine on the farm and sometimes feed animals or do little tasks. Especially the oldest son loves to ride tractors and be involved in the different activities that keep the farm running.

There is very little exchange with the outside world. The children have certain programs that they are allowed to watch. Their main television time however is spent watching approved videos, preferably so called "Veggie Tales" that show the life of Jesus and different biblical stories with vegetables as the actors. They are being produced by a company that belongs to the religious network associated with James Dobson's Focus on the Family.

The books that they rent from the local library tend to have religious content, however, not exclusively. The children are not allowed to read Harry Potter books as they are believed to encourage witchcraft which is an art taught by Satan.

The contact that takes place with the secular world is limited to shopping trips, either to the local grocery stores or to a larger town about an hour away where bigger chain stores such as Target or Sears are available. Shelly has thus far refused to explain to her children that a local fast food restaurant has closed down and will re-open as a liquor store. She pretends to know nothing about the new owners. She was shocked to hear that her husband used to drink alcohol while in college and equals people that do drink moderate amounts of alcohol with alcoholics.

Shelly meets with other women once a month along with her mother and her grandmother when they attend "Christian Women" which is a sort of club that usually provides lunch, a program usually with a motivational religious speaker, prayer and some hymnal singing.

Her political standpoint is conservative which is based solely on the pro-life/pro-choice debate. She felt uninvolved when September 11th happened since she was so far away from where it happened.

1.2. The Religious Right and Neo-conservatism

In this chapter I will explore the relationship between the Religious Right and U.S. Neo-conservatism including the New Right. While in American and Anglo-Saxonian literature the term "Neo-conservatism" is often limited to neo-conservative intellectuals, others such as Fetscher (1983) or Loesche (1982) go further and include the New Right into this scheme. Both neo-conservative intellectuals and members of the populist oriented New Right form parts of the new American conservatism on the basis of cultural and political elites. Both draw their beliefs from the political and cultural values and tradition of the United States although their backgrounds are very different. They dissociate themselves from the "Old Right" and have entered a "working alliance" (Minkenberg 1990: 148) since the beginning of the 1980's.

1.2.1. Neo-conservatism and the New Right

The conservatism that became prominent with the 1964 presidential campaign of Barry Goldwater resulted in a mobilization of various groups of evangelicals who previously did not tend to take part in politics. Goldwater's conservatism was different than the Midwestern "main street" conservatism and the elite intellectual conservatism of the 1940's and 1950's. It was rooted in a deep distrust from the Southern and Western part of the United States against the Northeastern political establishment and its liberalism. According to political analyst Kevin Phillips, it "represented an insurgency, not an attempt at traditional Republican preservationism" (Phillips1983: 57).

Although Goldwater lost the campaign, this type of populist conservatism grew rapidly on what Phillips calls the "two decade breakdown" of the 1960's and 1970's (Phillips 1983: 58). The breakdown described included moral and social changes as well as the perception of a declining economy and military, a decline in public institutions and diplomatic weakness. It was a new type of conservatism that Phillips calls "center extremism".

"[It] fitted neither liberal nor conservative prescriptions but linked the economics of frustration with indignant social conservatism and suspicion of rich and poor alike.[...It was] a reaction of traditionalism, (white) ethnicity, pro-family sentiment and religious fundamentalism – a Counter Reformation on the heels of the Reformation" (Phillips 1983: 58).

However, Goldwater, as Maidens (1982: 66) writes, did not agree with the emerging Neo-conservatism. He did not even see the term "conservative" as legitimate: "I'm frankly sick and tired of the political preachers across this country telling me as a citizen that, if I want to be a moral person, I must believe in A, B, C, or D... I don't like the New Right. What they are talking about is not conservatism".

Although leaders, such as Paul Weyrich and Richard Viguerie, of this "New Right" as they called themselves were using the label "conservative", the new movement was not aimed at preserving the status quo. Quite the opposite holds true. The New Right made it very clear that there were major differences between the less effective older forms of conservatism and their own attempt at politics. The New Right was not trying to "conserve" society as it was, rather the goal was to go back in time and reach the *status quo ante* of fifteen, twenty-five or even sixty years earlier in cultural and moral terms while aiming at a more modern approach for economical matters (Watson 1997: 20).

This approach of looking backwards was especially appealing to the fundamentalist-evangelical people who were attempting to preserve the religion, culture and morals of late nineteenth-century America. Historian Fritz Stern calls this a "revolutionary conservatism" (1961: xvi).

"[It seeks] to destroy the despised present in order to recapture an idealized past in an imaginary future...They sought a breakthrough to the past, and they longed for a new community in which old ideals and institutions would once again command universal allegiance"

However, it took more than a decade for evangelicals to enter the political arena. Ironically, this did not happen with the help of the conservatives or the Republican Party but with the election of Jimmy Carter to the presidency. He received the support of evangelicals in the 1976 election but by 1980 had disappointed many of his former supporters. Viguerie claims that Carter ignored the born again Christians and actively tried to hurt the

Christian movements in America (Viguerie 1980: 173; Watson 1997: 20). Furthermore, the positions of the Carter administration on abortion, prayer in schools, busing, the Equal Rights Amendment and gay rights did not coincide with those of the majority of evangelicals.

The appearance of the Religious Right as a political force soon led to accusations of trying to impose a broad uniformity on the American people. A brochure published by People for the American Way reads: "[T]heir declared goal is the enactment of laws that will prohibit everything which goes against their narrow interpretation of the will of God" (Watson 1997: 21).

The rejection of the public-private distinction is one of the basic features of the New Right. Legal scholar John H. Garvey calls this feature the "offensive agenda" (Watson 1997: 21). It includes trying to use the law for moral reformation of society. While modernity has defined evangelical morality and belief as private matters with no standing in public life, the New Right wants to restore their public role and authority to where it was in the late nineteenth century.

Furthermore, the expansion of various regulatory agencies of the federal government was perceived as an interference with personal matters and as an attack by the forces of modernity. Even beyond judicial decisions on school prayer and abortions, the expanding network of evangelical colleges or broadcasting enterprises, in their perception, was being threatened by the federal government through an increased regulation of family life and education. Nathan Glazer (1982: 250) wrote:

> "In other words, it is the great successes of secular and liberal forces, principally operating through the specific agency of the courts, that has in large measure created the issues on which the Fundamentalists have managed to achieve what influence they have."

The family, for the emerging movement of politicized evangelicals as well as for the cooperating New Right, became a term heavily infused with symbolism. The "ideal, traditional" American family was really a concept from the past: "The prototypical nineteenth-century bourgeois family" (Hunter in Watson 22/76). On a political, personal, religious and social level, the family was to be rescued from the influences of the cultural revolution of the sixties: Birth control, abortion, sexual revolution, no-fault divorce, feminist and gay-rights movements as well as the recognition of children's rights were, in the opinion of many of the New Right, immanent

First Chapter: Religious Right and Neo-conservatism

to the decline of the American family. Since the end of the nineteenth century, these topics were another manifestation of the "evil" influences that modernity had on society and culture. Furthermore, the topic of family provided a common ground with those members of the political right that were not in the evangelical or fundamentalist religious movements.

For many members of the Religious Right, the threat to the family was made even more visible by the highly symbolical decision of the Supreme Court in Roe vs. Wade[15]. The writer Francis Schaeffer provided evangelicals with a dualistic intellectual framework in which abortion was the inhuman result of materialistic humanism which he claims to be the antithesis of theistic Christianity. In his very influential works traditional evangelical morality, the opposition to abortion, hostility towards secular modernity and the perception of America as a Christian nation before God all came together in an appeal to the evangelical public to get engaged in political action. Evangelical scholar Ronald H. Nash wrote that "[m]ore than anything else, Schaeffer's influence may have led conservative evangelicalism to embark on a crusade to turn America around" (Nash 1987: 22).

America itself became another symbolical battleground. More than anything, in the eyes of the Religious Right, America was under attack from outside forces like the international threat of communism and, equally or even more so, from national forces. Moral and religious corruption, which were once again believed to be the result of the social revolution of the sixties, were the triggers for many national sins which were faithfully pointed out by the leaders of the Religious Right and followed by a call for national repentance[16].

However, premillennialist preachers such as Jerry Falwell were heavily contradicting themselves by urging evangelicals to get involved in politics and to take action. Up until this point, the patient waiting for the imminent

---

[15] Roe vs. Wade marked the 1973 Supreme Court decision legalizing abortion (Diamond 1998: 63)
[16] If we look at the comments that Falwell made concerning the September 11th attacks, the rhetoric has stayed the same:
"*God continues to lift the curtain and allows the enemies of America to give us probably what we deserve...The pagans and the abortionists and the feminists and the gays and the lesbians who are actively trying to make that an alternative lifestyle, the ACLU, People for the American Way - all of them who have tried to secularize America - I point the finger in their face and say, 'You helped this happen.'*"
The Rev. Jerry Falwell speaking with Pat Robertson on "The 700 Club", September 13. Robertson immediately responded, "*Well, I totally concur.*" (www.pfaw.org)

return of Christ in order for Him to establish His kingdom was the usual creed of premillennialist evangelicals. According to Watson (1997: 23) "[i]f anything, the logic of Premillennialism dictated an outsider role in relation to a culture and a political system that was about to be destroyed by God's wrath". Clearly, this outsider role was not what was thought of when urging evangelicals to take political action.

According to Marsden (1991: 81), for many Religious Right evangelicals there is an insider identification with American culture and politics that does not have premillennialism as the most influential factor to it. The "Christian Right's jeremiad"[17], as Watson (1997: 23) calls it, is mainly due to the fact that Religious Right evangelicals are mourning the loss of cultural dominance. The memory of it results in a wish for restoring this dominance and in a perception of themselves as the, as Wacker (Watson 1997: 82) names it, "custodians" of the culture. Many hold the view that there is a national covenant with God which is engaged in deuteronomic interpretations of American history and that through Religious Right evangelicals and their faith, the entire country can be saved. Evangelical authors Peter Marshall and David Manuel word it as follows:

> "Our forefathers have broken the trail for us, and shown the way. Their call is our call. If just a fraction of us Americans choose to go the Covenant Way, it will suffice. " (Watson 1997: 83)

This restoration of a covenanted Christian America has been present in Religious Right literature for a long time and is one of the major themes. This attempt at recapturing an idealized past for an imaginary future has also been one of the basic pillars of the Religious Right's "revolutionary conservatism".

The materialization of the Religious Right came as something of a surprise, at least to the mainstream observers of politics and religion in the United States. As late as the sixties, leading evangelical theologians such as Carl F.H. Henry had claimed that the involvement in government and politics would be connected to the negative role that government was playing in society and that true improvement of a society could only be achieved by means of individual spiritual cleansing. This reflected the classic liberal

---

[17] I will use the terms "Christian Right" and "Religious Right" interchangeably in this paper.

tradition of Americanism and the orthodox positions of Protestantism of the late 19th century. However, during the seventies, movement leaders such as Falwell started theologically legitimizing the involvement with more secular institutions and political processes. He put emphasis on such terms as "Christian civilization" or "Bible commonwealth" which in turn led to associations with the early American puritan vision of the "City upon the Hill" [18]. By combining these religious motives along with political ones, Falwell and others started using theocratic rhetoric which, for the audience, legitimized the involvement in political processes.

Due to this surrender to political involvement, leaders of the evangelical and fundamentalist churches and the New Right could start working together on issues that they were mutually interested in. According to Minkenberg (1990: 124), political leaders such as Viguerie or Weyrich helped the Religious Right form organizations whose goal was to channel religiously motivated people into members of a political process. At the beginning of the 1980's, there were about ninety organizations of the Religious Right which were concerned with mobilizing the grass-roots, establishing direct-mail listings and forming task forces dealing with topics such as education, research or training. Pat Robertson's Christian Broadcasting Network (CBN) has been a viable instrument in broadcasting programs and collecting donations for these organizations. This is contrary to when Robertson founded the Christian Coalition where almost all of the donation quests were only centered on that particular organization. The three early organizations that were channeling much of the constituency and financial powers were the Moral Majority, the Religious Roundtable and the Christian Voice. None of them are still active today but only the Moral Majority has been officially dissolved (Wilcox 2000). The Christian Coalition picked up many of the constituents of the Moral Majority, and Jerry Falwell is a frequent guest on Robertson's The 700 Club.

Interestingly, the political leaders, although supporting religious leaders in their efforts, neither share the religious faith nor the life style of the religious leaders or their constituents. However, the main perception that the U.S. is in the middle of a moral and cultural crisis and the failure of the establishment to deal with the issues are very motivational reasons for working together with the New Right.

---

[18] "The City upon a Hill" was meant to stand above everything else, to be a model society that lived a life according to the will of God with prosperity for all and goes back to Longfellow.

The sudden emergence, the harsh rhetoric and figures such as Jerry Falwell[19] has led to the appearance of another group of activists: Those critical of the Religious Right. Their rhetoric has been similar to those they disagree with and has led to a highly publicized and hysterical public discourse at times. All in all, the perception of the Religious Right has a negative connotation to it, in part, due to this type of communication. Some of the main topics for many people within as well as outside the Religious Right are still remaining. They are very emotionally charged topics which are difficult to have objective discussions about. However, many people outside the Religious Right show some sympathy towards the concerns expressed on social and moral matters, but the negative image of the Religious Right and some of its more extreme rhetoric[20] have kept many members of the mainstream from supporting their cause.

Conclusion

It is difficult to draw clear distinctions between the Neo-conservatives, the New Right and the Religious Right. They all have one thing in common: they perceive that the United States is in a deep cultural crisis. In order to combat this crisis they believe it is necessary to go back to the status quo ante of about sixty years ago.

While the Neo-conservatives have a more intellectual approach and are part of the establishment in Washington, the New Right is working with a populist approach to show that they are "for the people". They both perceive religion to be an instrument and a framework that can help get society back on the "right path". Their aims are focused on the state of society.

The New Christian or Religious Right also believe that the status quo ante is desirable. However, they believe that religion and the relationship to God are the most important issue. By working on a close relationship with God and following his laws which is perceived as the most important thing, society will "heal" as a by-product. Although the state of society will be a nice side effect for members of the Religious Right, the individual relationship to God is deemed to be much more important.

---

[19] For more information on selected figures of the Religious Right see chapter 4.
[20] The radicalization of rhetoric that occurred during the Lewinsky/Clinton scandal on the Republican side, lead by members of the Religious Right, did not result in removing Clinton from the presidency. Many members of the mainstream Republicans grew tired of the process that Kenneth Starr was heading and heavily criticized the use of tax money for such an operation.

New Right, Religious Right and Neo-conservatives are working together, because they want to achieve similar goals; however, they are different groups with different interests.

1.2.2. Ideology

As mentioned above, representatives of the New Right and the Neo-conservatives claim that the American nation was based on Christian principles and that the abandonment of these principles has led to a weakening of the nation. In order to counteract these negative influences, these principles have to be reinstated, and the global spread of atheism and communism has to be resisted and turned around. According to Jerry Falwell, the task of the United States is to convert the rest of the world in order to stop moral and social decline:

> "The USA is without a doubt the greatest and most influential nation in the world. We have the people and the resources to evangelize the world in our generation" (Falwell 1986: 212).

The socio-cultural program forms the core of the New Right's ideology[21]. It is also the base for further actions and plans. According to Minkenberg (1990: 127), selectively cited polls act as an instrument for claiming that the majority of Americans agree on a broad conservative consensus. The polls include questions of sexuality, abortion, work ethics, traditional families, school prayer, laws that regulate the consumption of alcohol and drugs, violence on TV, etc.

By linking the perceived crisis of the nation to these socio-cultural factors and including the omnipresent threat of secular humanism and the left, the leaders of the Religious Right come to the conclusion that it is not economic problems that have led to the state that society is in today, but mainly that socio-cultural circumstances are to blame and take a top priority position for many Americans.

Weyrich, who sees a difference between the New Right and his own cultural conservatism which, nonetheless, are very similar, holds the social

---

[21] In this paper, the term "Ideology" will be based on Plamenatz' definition, calling an ideology 'a family of concepts' that is loosely used to describe concepts such as Liberalism and Conservatism. See also Bealy, Frank in *The Blackwell Dictionary of Political Science*.

First Chapter: Religious Right and Neo-conservatism

movements that have emerged from the sixties responsible for the crises that are taking place in the United States today:

> "We believe that there is an unbreakable link between traditional Western, Judeo-Christian values and the secular success of Western societies. These values which include definitions of right and wrong and ways of thinking and living have brought about the prosperity, liberty and opportunity for fulfillment that Western societies have offered their citizens. These will be lost if we abandon these values...There is a close, causal link between the abandonment of traditional ways of thinking and living since about 1960 and the national decline that has marked the same period" (Weyrich 1986: C4F).

The New Right is especially criticizing the American feminist movement and its organization NOW (National Organization of Women). Their attempt at adding the Equal Rights Amendment (ERA) to the constitution has been battled against relentlessly by the New Right, especially by the Eagle Forum. Phyllis Schlaffly, the founder of the Eagle Forum, found support mainly in the South where the "horror scenario of career women neglecting children and spouse found a broad reception. Opposite to this image is the picture of the "new traditional woman" that the New Right is painting. This woman is "other oriented" and passes on culture and values by educating her children[22].

Other important issues include abortion and the so called "family issues". The abortion topic has brought conservative Protestants and Catholics closer together. The latter, being an important voting block for the Democratic Party, are a new found ally in the fight against abortion. Minkenberg claims that formerly apolitical groups within society have become emotionally involved by a crusade-like campaign funded by the New Right (1997: 128).

---

[22] In this context, the growing number of parents, especially women, who are home-schooling their children and the industry that stands behind it is worth mentioning. Leading figures of the Religious Right, e.g. Dr. James Dobson or Dr. Laura Schlessinger are urging parents on their daily radio broadcasts to take their children out of public schools and to start home-schooling them (March 28, 2002, http://www.family.org/fmedia/bcpast.cfm). In 2001 the U.S. Census Bureau said that home-schooling was "emerging as an important national phenomenon." About 2 million children were home-schooled at that particular point in time with numbers increasing to 15 to 20 percent annually. In comparison, about 50 million children attend public schools in the United States.

Sexuality, pornography and homosexuality, in short: family issues, are another area that the New Right concentrates on. There are new alliances, for example, in the anti-porno movement. Ironically, women's rights organizations have become new allies here.

1.2.3. The Religious Right and Education

The educational system provides the New Right with an institution that is a valuable agent in passing on values and norms. In a group that is led by Mel and Norma Gabler called the Educational Research Analysis, the members are going through textbooks aimed at students of public schools in order to find passages that are promoting "secular humanism". They then organize public pressure on the publishers in order to convince them to re-write these passages.

Jerry Falwell likes to denounce sex education in public schools as "academic pornography" (Falwell 1986: 199f). Another hot topic in the area of public schools is school prayer which has been banned from the classroom since the much debated Supreme Court decision in 1962/63 (Wilcox 2000) There have been campaigns to reinstate school prayer, but so far, they have not been able to mobilize a majority of voters.

Finally, the topic of teaching evolution vs. creation is another issue when it comes to public schools. Ever since the Scopes trial in 1925, the teachings of evolution have become more and more predominant, much to the dismay of the New Right (Wilcox 2000).

During the seventies, criticism towards the technical ages found supporters in the Religious Right who claimed that the decline of traditional values and authority could be traced back to the secular rationalism and the liberalization of the education system.

However, teaching evolution was not supposed to be substituted by going back to teaching creationism in schools; they were supposed to be put on an equal level. Several organizations claimed that the so called "Creation Science" going back to Genesis was a scientific approach which was superior to the teachings of evolution.

The root of these programs can be seen in the public perception of the school system at the elementary and high school level which is seemingly becoming more and more secular and losing its quality. By forming a causal connection between these two links, the New Right finds a powerful legitimization for its cause and provides a seemingly simple solution: To reinstate a cognitive orientation framework based on religion and the "old values" (Minkenberg 1997: 130). By using governmental instruments in doing so, the New Right breaks away from the Old Right and tries to soften the constitutional separation of church and state. However, by using these governmental instruments, it also leads fundamentalists onto a new path: Getting involved in politics is a very new concept for many of them.

1.2.4. The Religious Right and Governmental Involvement

By Religious Right standards, government is supposed to be based on biblical examples and to set and enforce bliblical moral norms:

> "Fact-mongering and value-free scientific analysis have failed to cure our problems and have often been part of their cause. We believe that America has to look to values if it wants to solve the specific problems that confront it. Government has an important role in upholding the society's moral fabric – by its own example; by its use of the 'bully pulpit' inherent in government; and, sometimes, by legislation" (Weyrich 1986: C4F).

Government is also supposed to reform its judiciary branch: decisions about abortion, school busing, and administration of prisons or racial issues are supposed to be dealt with on the state or on an even more local level.

This concept, to bring decisions of this kind onto a state level, reflects a populist point of view and can be traced back to a dichotomous look at the world. According to Minkenberg (1990), this black-white thinking can also be found in the teachings of religious fundamentalists. Secular humanism, hereby, is being presented by the elite in politics, economy, education, administration, media and unions. The simple people stand opposite to this and are the "moral majority" of Middle Class America that see themselves as victims of the establishment.

The leaders of the Religious Right such as Weyrich and Viguerie are quick to point out their simple upbringing and the low formal level of education they received in order to make it clear which side they are on. They argue against the establishment or, to be more precise, against the establishment of today and, to be even more precise, against the liberal establishment:

"I am not anti-establishment per se... I have no problem with the establishment. It is this establishment that is working against the best interest of the people which concerns me. You take two hundred years ago; our country had a wonderful establishment" (Viguerie 1981).

In the eyes of the New Right, the political elite that is concentrated on the east coast is responsible for the spiritual and moral crisis that has occurred in the United States. Their solution is to put the power back into the people's hands and to go back to the grass-roots by forming a broad coalition on the base of a conservative consensus. The ideas of morals and norms are supposed to be the links that unite the middle and the working class and that will take over the system of "interest group liberalism".

1.2.5. Democratic Values

Since the New Right claims to stand for more direct democracy, the topic of national referenda plays an important role. Weyrich (1984: 227) argues that the model of an issue-oriented grass-roots democracy should be used for ordinary legislation as well as for changes or amendments to the constitution. He states that most of the states already demand referenda for changes of the constitution and that clever campaigns can manipulate not only the simple people but also the political elites. In his opinion, a legislation that is connected to an initiative will receive more research and discussion than an "ordinary" legislative campaign.

Minkenberg argues that the aim for a national referendum based on a conservative majority in the U.S. population for "social issues" poses the question of safeguarding minority positions as well as the question of the constitutional separation of church and state. In his opinion, Weyrich and others leave this question unanswered or point to the "un-American" character of secular humanism. In this context, Minkenberg comes to the conclusion that further democratization for the New Right does not present a value in itself, but is supposed to be used to re-evangelize the country. The political process is aimed at making the values and norms as well as the spiritual beliefs of the Religious Right binding for all Americans. The existing elite are supposed to be replaced with new elite which will consist of members of the New Right which is not supposed to aim at further democratization (1990: 131ff.)

First Chapter: Religious Right and Neo-conservatism

Many organizations of the New Right and the Religious Right in particular make it very clear that they believe in strong leaders and strong measures to give these leaders power[23]. Capital punishment, for example, is an idea that is vastly popular with members of the New Right despite the fact that from a biblical perspective, capital punishment is at the least questionable[24]. In this context, further democratization does not seem very probable. By looking at the rhetoric and actions taken by the Religious Right such as the ban of homosexuals in Colorado from certain civil rights by Amendment 2 which was later overruled by the Supreme Court on May 20, 1996, one can come to the conclusion that once in power, the Religious Right will aim at less democracy to maintain its status quo[25].

1.2.6. International Politics

In Foreign Politics the New Right found another area where it makes decisions on the basis of a dichotomist point of view. It is good vs. evil when the leaders of the New Right are trying to explain any conflict.

Israel plays an important role in foreign politics for the Religious Right[26]. Not only is it surrounded by non democratic Arabic governments and, therefore, plays an important strategic role, it is also important due to its role in the Old Testament. The question of a Palestine State is being completely ignored by the New Right. The state of Israel in its current and ancient form is a prerequisite for the Second Coming of Christ and the majority of members of the Religious Right are not in favor of the State of Palestine

---

[23] For examples of organizations of the Religious Right such as Focus on the Family, Family Research Council, Promise Keepers, etc. see Chapter 4.

[24] See: Ten Commandments, Maria of Magdala, a.s.o.

[25] Text of Colorado State Constitution Amendment 2 (Voted on and passed by a majority of Colorado voters in 1992): "No Protected Status Based on Homosexual, Lesbian, or Bisexual Orientation. Neither the State of Colorado, through any of its branches or departments, nor any of its agencies, political subdivisions, municipalities or school districts, shall enact, adopt or enforce any statute, regulation, ordinance or policy whereby homosexual, lesbian or bisexual orientation, conduct, practices or relationships shall constitute or otherwise be the basis of or entitle any person or class of persons to have or claim any minority status, quota preferences, protected status or claim of discrimination. This Section of the Constitution shall be in all respects self-executing."

[26] For statements concerning the developments around the middle Eastern peace process, see www.heritage.org

Concept that George W. Bush has proposed. Members of the neo-conservative think tank "Heritage Foundation" call the massacre of Jenin a "big lie" (Cohen http://www.heritage.org/views/2002 /ed041802.html) and battle for increased financial support of the Israeli Arrow Missile Defense program (http://www.heritage.org/views/2002/ed041802.html). Certainly such support cannot compromise U.S. Defense spending as Spring makes clear in his article.

Ever since the 1980's when the Soviet Union was one of the most prevalent enemies of the New Right, Jerry Falwell has been complaining about the loss of predominance for the United States:

"America is in serious trouble today. It has lost its economic and military prominence among the nations of the world. Exercising influence and leadership from this weakened position is an exercise in futility. Our leaders are finally realizing what many have tried to state for years: that the Soviets are liars and cheaters and that they are determined to conquer our free country and to infiltrate the American people with godless communism" (Falwell 1986: 213).

The United Nations is also a hot topic for the members of the Religious Right. Suggestions concerning this topic range from leaving the United Nations to not contributing to them financially anymore. This is not meant to further isolate the United States from the rest of the world, it is instead aimed at making the U.S. more flexible in dealing with global issues which in turn, however, will lead to further isolation. Pursuing American values such as freedom, equality or defending your own property are supposed to be easier without the U.N. Capitalism and Democracy, as the New Right interprets them, provide cultural values which, in the eyes of the Religious Right, should be aimed for by all nations. Unilateral[27] Globalism is the strategy to reach all these goals-a point of view that today's Bush administration seems to share. In the weeks after the September 11th

---

[27] Only after September 11th did Colin Powell, whose aims have been more multi-lateral, get another shot at being a public figure and speaker for the Bush administration. Ironically, Time Magazine had titled the issue that was published on September 10th, "Where are you Colin Powell?', commenting on the absence of Colin Powell at official appearances. Condoleezza Rice, Bush's security advisor and a strong force behind the United States becoming more uni-lateral, disappeared for the first few weeks after September 11th. As Bush was talking about allies and friends in other countries, Rice was apparently too much of a contradiction to be present at press conferences or public appearances where she could have been asked some questions concerning her stands.

attacks, the neo-conservative groups in Washington appeared to have gained more influence. In addition, the invasion of Iraq bears the handwriting of the neo-conservatives.

Before the fall of the Soviet Union, the New Right tried to continue where the McCarthy-Era had left off: Moralization of international relations such as describing the Soviet Union as a superior military power and the suspicion that the liberal establishment was not being anti-communist enough continued. However, its missionary role for the world extended that of the McCarthy-Era. The huge defense budget was accepted because of the role the United States was going to play in the Christianization of other countries. Apparently, the military seemed to be an instrument that could be used for that purpose (Minkenberg 1997: 140). The same pattern can be applied to the Iraq war in 2003. In any other department, such a tremendous budget allocation would have been intervened by the religious right since anything that stands for "big government" is heavily criticized.

After the Soviet Union disappeared, the Religious Right concentrated its foreign policy focus on the Middle East and the United Nations. The quote by Pines from 1984 still holds true for a large percentage within the Religious Right today:

> "A world without a United Nations – or without U.S. participation in a U.N. – in sum would be a world less hostile to the U.S. and the free enterprise system. More important, it would be a world which offers more hope to Third World Nations of democratic development and economic growth" (Pines 1984: 200).

Today's standpoint on the United Nations is not very different from that of the 1980's. In 1998, Bret Schaefer, member of the "Heritage Foundation", a New Right think tank, wrote a paper on "The International Criminal Court: Threatening U.S. Sovereignty and Security" which describes many of the points that the Bush administration is using against the international criminal court. Schaefer describes how an international criminal court would undermine the U.S. authority and would even threaten constitutional rights for U.S. citizens.

> "This unprecedented power could affect profoundly the rights guaranteed every American by the U.S. Constitution and threaten the ability of the United States to engage in military action to protect its national security interests. Because the ICC offers the United States no tangible benefits to outweigh these

egregious threats, Congress and the Clinton Administration should strongly oppose it" (Schaefer 1998:1).

In a lecture given at the International Symposium on the United States and the United Nations: "Exploring the Future of U.S. - U.N. Relations", Schaefer draws an outline of how he imagines the relationship between the U.N. and the U.S. should be (Schaefer 1998). He sees the U.N. as an enemy rather than as a partner and believes the United States should concentrate on unilateralism. If the United Nations plans are according to U.S. strategy, Schaefer is happy to "[welcome] U.N. support through Security Council resolutions and General Assembly declarations. Though not strictly necessary, this support provided valuable diplomatic and economic support for America's war on terrorism". According to Schaefer the "war on terrorism" poses an exception to the rule where international support is welcome. Allies can be helpful to the U.S. when it comes to things such as over flight permissions or logistical support. However, Schaefer makes it clear that the U.S. **could** go alone if necessary, and any involvement of the United Nations or particular countries will be subject to the U.S. rules.

However, for the New Right, protecting America's national interests seems to be more so a case of protecting one particular national interest: keeping the wealthy people satisfied. The low level representatives that were sent to the "*World Conference against Racism, Racial Discrimination, Xenophobia, and Related Intolerance*" were, according to Schaefer, a sign of protest against issues surrounding compensation for slavery. If the Religious Right was really pro equality and pro justice for all, certainly this very dark chapter of American history would be dealt with. However, by denying the attention this conference deserved, the New Right made clear whose interests it really wants to protect.

1.2.7. Shared Values of the New Right and Neo-Conservatives

As mentioned above, neo-conservatives and the New Right share the perception of the deep crisis of the society of the United States and western countries in general. They consider the trigger of this crisis to be an excess of democracy and "social engineering". A dichotomous view of the world identifies those that profit most from these processes: secular humanists and those behind the changes that have taken place since the sixties and seventies. In foreign politics the distinction between friend and enemy becomes even clearer. Neo-conservatives and the New Right are for an unconditional support of Israel (for different motivations) and were clearly anti-communist during the cold war era. The foreign policy of the second Bush administration is dominated by neo-conservatives who already published papers in the late nineties about Saddam Hussein and matters in the Middle East (Boelsche 2000). Vice-President Cheney and Secretary of Defense Rumsfeld are among those neo-conservatives. This is characterized by an aggressive foreign policy that is trying to reduce the influence of the United Nations by not adhering to international law.

Both sides emphasize the importance of the Judeo-Christian tradition of the Western hemisphere which primarily shows how the Moral Majority tried to appeal to the Jewish electorate. In the beginning, the Moral Majority was branded as somewhat anti-Semitic, and Irving Kristol and Jerry Falwell tried hard to diminish that impression. They did so by claiming that the Jewish population should give up their traditional affinity to the post-New Deal-Liberalism and switch to neo-conservative politics (Kristol 1984).

Kristol states that neo-conservatism is not just a product of intellectual elites but that the closeness to the American people is what distinguishes it from other ideologies and concepts. With the emphasis on populism, he is building a "golden bridge" for the New Right which is traditionally a more populist movement.

According to Minkenberg, Weyrich is a "bridge builder" for the New Right. He claims that the program that Kristol presents in regard to neo-conservatism can be applied to the New Right as well (1997: 156).

Furthermore, neo-conservatism and the New Right are in accordance when it comes to politics and morals in the United States. Homosexuality and abortion are being condemned, however, legalization of abortion in severe cases such as rape or the endangerment of the life of the mother appears to be widely accepted. The decision about school prayer should be left up to the local community, however, voluntary school prayer should not be forbidden. Generally, religious pluralism seems to be accepted although the emphasis still lies on the Judeo-Christian heritage.

The consensus in some questions should not hide that there are indeed still differences between the two tendencies within the New Conservatives.

The neo-conservatives play the dominant role in the Bush administration today. In 1997, a group of the most influential neo-conservatives founded the "Project for the New American Century" (PNAC). In their preamble they are demanding the preservation and expansion of American dominance in Europe and Asia in particular. In order to do so, an increase in military spending to 3.8% of the GDP is being advised. Anything but the support of the hegemonic character of the United States is detrimental and not in the interest of the United States.

> "Over the past decade, the neo-cons have argued that the United States should challenge evil regimes in the Mideast and Asia, spread freedom, democracy and capitalism, jettison Cold War thinking based on deterrence and containment, and de-emphasize old treaties and alliances that get in the way" (Eric Black, Star Tribune).

Ten of the twenty-five signing founders of the PNAC hold important positions in the Bush administration today or are close consultants. These are:

- Richard B. Cheney is Vice President of the United States
- Lewis Libby is Chief of Staff for Richard B. Cheney
- Donald Rumsfeld is Secretary of Defense
- Paul Dundes Wolfowitz is Vice-Secretary of Defense
- Peter W. Rodman is responsible for international matters of security
- John Bolton is State Secretary for Control of Armament
- Richard Armitage is Vice-Secretary of State
- Richard Perle, who used to be Vice Secretary of Defense under Reagan, was head of the American Defense Policy Board but had to resign in 2003 for connecting private business with his office.
- William Kristol is the head of the PNAC and acts as the "brain of the President"
- Zalmay Khalilzad is, after he was special ambassador to Afghanistan, Bush's special contact to the Iraqi opposition

First Chapter: Religious Right and Neo-conservatism

The Neo-conservatives hold key positions in the Bush administration along with some members of the Religious Right (e.g. Ashcroft). They have reached an unprecedented influence in American politics, and they have been able to have these successes, because the Religious Right and the New Right are allies and have been working closely together.

1.3. Aspects of the History of the Religious Right

1.3.1. Early Beginnings

Undoubtedly, the United States has a long history of religious movements. Since much of the cultural and political development of the society has been closely tied to the principles of the founding fathers, many believe that although there is a separation of church and state, this separation has been threatened by the Religious Right. The Religious Right, on the other hand, believes that the former religious orientation of many leaders and of the society as a whole has succumbed to "secular humanism" which will lead society into being destructed at best and being led by the devil at worst. The awareness of this history helps to understand the climate and agenda of the New Religious Right as it is today. This chapter aims to cover the more important phases in the development of the Religious Right over the last century and the last two decades in particular.

The USA was formerly a protestant country where "colonial religion generally derived from the tenets of protestant Reformation" (Carrol and Noble 1982: 62). Many of the first settlers were very conscious protestants which immigrated to America in order to live their religion. In 1830 there were only about 300,000 Catholics (Carrol and Noble 1982: 179) in the United States. The great diversity of all the other immigrants created a very heterogeneous landscape within Protestantism.

In the last quarter of the 19th century, many religious leaders tried to adapt the traditional views to modern scientific findings. This was counteracted by people that viewed these adaptations as heresy.

In the first two decades of the twentieth century, traditionalists were writing essays that were supposed to stop this kind of heresy. Among the more important ones was a series of short essays written between 1910 and 1915 which were called the "Fundamentals[28]". The inerrancy and literal

---

[28] The Fundamentals contained ninety essays on a wide variety of topics. Many of the writers were distinguished teachers that had earned doctorates. It was a very diverse collection of topics, as some even came to the conclusion that any fundamentalist could adopt or reject Socialism as they saw fit. The aim of the series was to produce intellectually sound material for defending Christianity. The preface to the fifth edidtion stated that one of its aims was that "the unbelief, which in pulpit and pew has been paralyzing the Church of Christ, may be overcome, and that a world-wide revival may be the result." (Dixon 1915)

interpretation of the bible, Creationism and Prelimenniarism built the basis for this belief.

In the years after 1915 fundamentalism became more and more a social movement, falling on fertile ground nourished by the upheaval of the decades before WWI which had drastically increased the faith in prophecies. Three international Prophecy Conferences were held between 1914 and 1918 alone (Ammermann 1998: 76) where speakers examined the apocalyptic character of the times in connection to the premilleannial teachings of the previous decades.

The League of Nations evoked fears of a global government which, among the dispensationalists, was widely believed to be part of a tribulation to come. Also the growth of communism as an ideology without God was a sign of a tribulation to come for many people. The liberal protestants that placed an emphasis on global ecumenism in the postwar years scared the people that were concerned about national and doctrinal distinctions. The concerns of the fundamentalists matched the needs of parts of the society: They aimed at restoring the one true and sure belief and, by doing so, at keeping the nation strong.

After 1925 leaders of the fundamentalists started to have more heterogeneous views which lead to a weakening of the movement. With this loss of credibility, the ability to rally on a national or even denominational basis vanished. In the search for a new image for the USA, it became clear that it would not be based on an inerrant scripture. People that were still concerned with the "health" of the country were no longer taken seriously and did not gain wide public hearing.

Rather than a demise of the movement, a transformation and reorganization process began. Until 1925 the fundamentalist movement was widely seen as a group of people trying to restore Christian civilization and orthodox religion. After 1925 it became an outsider movement with its members changing their view on mainstream culture and religion. In many of their followers' opinion, the denominations were not better than the secular world due to their adaptation to an entire culture that was now influenced mainly by non-Christian beliefs. This exclusion of God lead to the term "secular humanism" which was widely used (Ammerman 1998: 82) from then on.

First Chapter: Religious Right and Neo-conservatism

The Scopes Trial[29] added another defeat to the fundamentalist movement, and hereafter, the group's primary strategy was more to save individual souls than to influence the masses.

The local missionary movements stemming from the fundamentalist churches usually took the form of an independent traveling missionary who would gather a community's conservatives together in an effort to save as many souls as possible. The likes of Bob Jones Sr.[30] and John R. Rice preferred to keep their evangelism pure from people like Billy Graham who was trying to win souls in a more ecumenical manner.

Another group that was targeted was the youth. Youth for Christ and Inter Varsity Christian Fellowship were fundamentalist ministries that grew quickly. Campus Crusade for Christ, founded by Bill Bright in 1951, was stationed on forty college campuses in 15 states by 1961 and gathered a large audience by its simplified gospel "Four Spiritual Laws[31]".

1.3.2. Fundamentalism

Fundamentalism offered comprehensive and satisfying explanations for life's complexities. People holding on to fundamentalism chose a life of certainty in a very uncertain world. The church offered a surrounding where everything still made sense and people were still living by the right rules. Because the local orientation of those churches offered real support in hard

---

[29] In 1925 John Scopes was charged for teaching evolution in Tennessee's public schools which was against a law that had just been passed. The American Civil Liberties Union sent a team of lawyers, headed by Clarence Darrow, to defend him while the anti-evolutionists were headed by William Jennings Bryan. The highly publicized trial between science and religion was decided in favor of the anti-evolutionists, but in the public eye it had become the defeat of the fundamentalists due to extensive and very negative media coverage.

[30] He is the founder of Bob Jones University, a highly controversial college with an agenda to the very right of the political spectrum. Up to this day the university makes clear to its students that interracial dating is not in the university's interest and according to their interpretation, unbiblical (Bruce 1988: 43). George W. Bush has been heavily criticized for giving a speech there during his campaign. He even had to write a letter of apology to Catholic leaders because of the University's strong anti-catholic history.

[31] Four spiritual laws: 1. God **LOVES** you and offers a wonderful **PLAN** for your life.
2. Man is **SINFUL** and **SEPARATED** from God. Therefore, he cannot know and experience God's love and plan for his life.
3. Jesus Christ is God's **ONLY** provision for man's sin. Through Him you can know and experience God's love and plan for your life.
4. We must individually **RECEIVE** Jesus Christ as Savior and Lord; then we can know and experience God's love and plan for our lives.

times, it became a social factor as well as a religious one. Since many of the established major northern organizations were now dominated by modernism, the remaining fundamentalists had to make a choice: To either stay with their denomination or consider separation. Many independent denominations and loose organizations stem from this time between the post war period and the 1950's, e.g. Independent Fundamental Churches of America (IFCA), the Baptist Bible Fellowship (BBF), American Council on Christian Churches (ACCC) or the National Association of Evangelicals (NAE).

The organizational structures stemmed back about a century (Ammerman 1998: 83) when people concerned about morals, evangelism and scripture frequently came together in revivals and conferences which eventually led to the activist movements of the post-war period.

Another important influence-to-come that was born during the time between 1920 and 1975 was the usage of the media. While a distinctive fundamentalist publishing network had already been existing fairly early in the process, now the radio and, in the fifties, television were starting to play a role in spreading the Word. In adapting their style to the medium of television, revivalists such as Billy Graham, Rex Humbard and Oral Roberts set the trend, recognizing the strong powers that this medium held. After the Federal Communications Commission began allowing paid time to count toward the stations' public service requirements, a surge of paid conservative religious broadcasts flooded the country. Ministries that concentrated on broadcasting grew quickly and soon replaced the Bible institutes and revivalists as the denominational centers of the movement.

Some of the fundamentalists turned to political and cultural radicalism, believing they were being threatened by conspiracy politics and communism. However, they did not represent the US religious conservatives of the time. In fact, many disagreed with the radical views of someone like Carl McIntire[32].

As the 1970's were approaching, fundamentalism in the United States could rely on a rich legacy of ideas, organizational forms and relationships with

---

[32] Carl McIntire, founder of the ACCC started to preach for radical anti communism in the beginning of the fundamentalist movement. However, in the Cold War era his concerns were taken more seriously by a much larger number of people. His tireless efforts against mainstream church leaders won him a spot among Senator Joseph McCarthy's helpers. He wrote lists of communist sympathizers among the clergy and claimed that the Revised Standard Version of the Bible was, in fact, a product of a Red plot (Ammerman 1998: 88f).

the larger world. The original role as a defender of orthodoxy was no longer in question.

Instead, it had turned into a cultural and religious battle for keeping that orthodoxy despite the success of modernism. When this battle could not be won either, the fundamentalist body split up and went in different directions. Some took their potential and built new organizations that rivaled the mainline denominations in institutional strength while others moved towards the mainstream in order to gain more influence by revising their status as outsiders.

A few went into politics in order to provide an ideological cleansing that they felt was necessary to lead the United States back to the Christian heritage that they presumed had been lost.

The social changes of the 60's and the experience that not all presidents of the United States were trust-worthy led to a certain urgency for getting the Christian heritage back. For many people this apparent disintegration of society made clear that the Rapture was near. As individuals often experience cultural change as an intolerable shaking of the foundations, people from a wide spectrum found their way into fundamentalist churches (Ammerman 1998: 91).

Culture, in general, seemed crazy for many people, and it was especially drastic in the South. Urbanization, industrialization and immigration came to the South about one century later than in the North.

People had been leaving their farms ever since the depression, but the speed picked up after World War II. Air conditioning and cheap labor made the region attractive for corporate moves and new ventures. Migration from other regions was larger than from small southern towns and farms. The environment created by the influence of these new-comers was, thus, far more pluralistic than before, and many southerners found themselves in a world they hardly recognized (Ammerman 1998: 92).

The social changes in the 1960's also changed the Democratic Party's grip on the South: With the party's embrace of civil rights issues, many traditional Southerners and many Democrats all over the country became more interested in morality and lifestyle issues which the Republicans could catch their attention with. Some people also thought about the churches for providing the grounds on which to decide these issues.

The retreat from Vietnam created new fears in some fundamentalist's minds. The U.S. saw a possible growth in communism and a decline of U.S. military and economic might. This would possibly harm their ability to evangelize the world. The "city upon a hill" chosen by God to lead the light of the Gospel was further endangered when the Supreme Court outlawed prescribed prayers in public schools in 1963. Over the next fifteen years, it became more and more clear to many fundamentalists that their religious beliefs and traditions were endangered and that the single ideological source for this endangerment was the secular humanists. Tim LaHaye's popular book, *The Battle for the Mind* (1980), stated some of the developments that many fundamentalists found difficult to tolerate. Among them were the following:

1. A constitutional amendment was proposed that could have been interpreted as an amendment to prevent women from fulfilling their biblical role as submissive wives, primarily in the household.

2. The family was further attacked as social agencies and legislatures sought to define the limits of physical punishment permitted in a father's attempt to discipline his children.

3. The IRS began to take on the task of investigating religious agencies' finances and determining what "counted" as true religion (at least for tax purposes).

4. Civil rights arguments began to be extended to those (especially homosexuals) whose lives fundamentalists deemed grossly immoral.

5. Not only could children not pray in school, they were also being taught "values clarification" and other "humanists" ideas that undermined the unwavering beliefs and traditions their parents held dear.

6. Even Christian schools could not do their work without government agencies imposing certification restrictions, which seemed to strip them of their theological power.

7. And finally, all the forces seeking to destroy traditional families and moral society seemed to converge in a court ruling, *Roe v Wade*, that found abortion a matter of private choice.

1.3.3. The Third Wave

A revived new fundamentalist Religious Right started to organize in the late 70's. This third wave of activity seems to have been precipitated mainly by two sets of events. A series of local political movements throughout the country demonstrated that fundamentalists and evangelists too can have political energy. In order to protest textbooks in the Kanawha County of West Virginia, to help repeal gay rights legislation in Dade County Florida and to oppose the Equal Rights Amendment (ERA) in numerous cities and states, many formerly inactive members of the Religious Right turned into activists (Wald 1987: 27).

The other influence on the new Religious Right was the presidential candidacy of Jimmy Carter who was a born-again Southern Baptist. Carter was a deeply religious man who was very involved with his church. His sister was an evangelist. He publicly called on evangelists to give up their distrust in politics and to become more involved which lead white evangelicals to vote in greater numbers than in past elections (Wilcox 2000: 36).

Conservative politicians realized at this point that fundamentalists and other evangelicals could actually be induced to vote in larger numbers and recognized the potential of having these people vote Republican. By the end of the decade, conservative leaders provided resources in order to help build up groups such as the Religious Roundtable, the Christian Voice and the religious group that attracted the most attention, the Moral Majority[33] (Moen 1992: 56).

The Moral Majority's leader was Jerry Falwell who was a Baptist Bible Fellowship pastor. He had built a Mega Church in Lynchburg, Virginia, with 15,000 members and then had his sermons televised as the Old Time Gospel Hour on more than 300 stations (Wilcox 2000: 36). He was an eager advocate for the Religious Right and appeared soon after Ronald Reagan's victory in the 1980 election in order to claim that the Religious Right was the one to thank for the conservative's win. However, since the recruited local leaders of the Moral Majority were mainly pastors from within the Baptist Bible Fellowship (BBF) who were not exactly known to be the most tolerant toward Catholics, Pentecostals, Charismatics, Evangelicals and mainline Protestants, it was difficult to find activists for the local chapters that would actually go out and initiate activities (Wilcox 2000: 37).

---

[33] See also chapter 2

These newly founded religious groups had much broader agendas than the ones before them. The main issues included the opposition to abortion, to civil rights protection for gays and lesbians, to the ERA as well as support for school prayer and tuition tax credits for religious schools. In addition to this, Falwell made a highly publicized defense of South African Politics and the increase in defense spending. The organization's newsletter, the "Moral Majority Report" took viewpoints on conservative issues and supported a sub minimum wage, a return to the gold standard and cuts in social welfare spending.

According to Clyde Wilcox (Wilcox 2000), 10 to 15 percent of the American public supported the Religious Right. However, their fate was determined by the direct-mail revenues which these organizations financed themselves with, and times became more difficult.

> "By the mid-1980's, it became increasingly harder for these groups to induce the primarily elderly women who constituted their financial base to part with their money" (Wilcox 2000: 37).

There were two main reasons for the slower flow of donation money. First of all, the re-election campaign held by Ronald Reagan claimed that it was already "morning in America" which meant that the president had supposedly already succeeded in re-establishing America's historical values. Therefore, the actual need to send money in order to "save" America became less urgent.

The second reason was a series of scandals involving televangelists in the late 80's. The increasingly frequent appeals for money made many more people skeptical about the Religious Right. This was topped off by Oral Roberts' statement that God would "call him home" if Roberts did not succeed in raising several million dollars from contributions by viewers in order to keep his ministry going. The Bakker[34] scandal did not help to increase the credibility of the Religious Right although neither the Bakkers' nor Oral Roberts' ministries were openly politically active.

These incidents made it much more difficult for the Moral Majority to raise money, and after being in financial difficulties in 1988, it was disbanded in

---

[34] Jim Bakker eventually served time in prison in the late 1980's for fraud, after being accused of various improprieties in connection with sexual and financial matters. It was also reported that he and his wife had gold fixtures in their bathroom and an air-conditioned doghouse for their dog (Wilcox 2000),

1989. Jerry Falwell announced that he quit, because the goals of the Moral Majority had been met. In reality, the key issues up to this date still remained open. He announced in 1999 that he was thinking about creating another organization in order to follow in the footsteps of the Moral Majority, but so far, nothing has happened, and the internet address currently leads to a Christian filter for websites.

Conclusion

The Third Wave of the Christian Fundamentalist Movement hit the United States after the social changes of the 1960's. At the end of the 1970's, evangelicals were becoming more politically active, first under President Jimmy Carter, then under President Ronald Reagan for the Republicans. The resulting Religious Right movement gained considerable momentum in the 1980' despite the fact that it had to endure a serious of setbacks. Professionalization made them major players in the political arena.

1.3.4. The Robertson Candidacy

Another major player of the Religious Right is Marion "Pat" Robertson who announced in 1987 that he would run for the Republican presidential nomination. He had never held an elected office but, nevertheless, had been active in politics for over a decade and also built a very successful business empire.

Robertson was the host of "The 700 Club" which was a religious talk show on television where a variety of guests talked about their faith and shared music and religious experiences. The show also offered a conservative analysis of the political landscape. The financial base for his presidential nomination campaign was mainly laid out by the viewers of this show. Many of them joined the "1988 Club" which meant they had to contribute regular gifts of $19.88. Robertson's political topics included the failure of the American education system, the opposition to abortion, anti-communism and the idea of "a year of Jubilee" based on the Old Testament during which debt would be forgiven[35].

Robertson beat George Bush for second place in the Iowa caucuses, but beyond that, a series of negative stories hurt his campaign and made him the object of widespread public ridicule. During this time, televangelist Jimmy Swaggart was caught in a motel room with a prostitute which turned out to

---

[35] A closer look at Pat Robertson's ideas will be taken in chapter 4.

be an act of revenge by a fellow televangelist although Robertson claimed that it was a dirty trick by the Bush campaign. The public was once again reminded of the Oral Roberts and Jim and Tammye Bakker scandals and voted accordingly. Another drawback for the Robertson campaign was the fact that the Moral Majority was limited in its outreach to other religious groups. Since Robertson was a Pentecostal, many members of the mainly Baptist Moral Majority were less likely to vote for him than mainline protestants. Robertson tried to involve African-Americans and Catholics, but both groups did not vote often in Republican Primaries.

Robertson ended up spending more money campaigning than any other candidate ever had and still failed to win a single primary. He lost badly, even in his home state of Virginia.

However, the presidential nomination campaign was an important cornerstone in establishing a new, more sophisticated Religious Right. The Robertson activists continued making an influence by selecting the delegates for the national convention. They were pledged by state law to vote for Bush but actually supported Robertson and worked on a local level to gain influence in state and local party committees.

In 1989, Robertson continued to work, but his organization had a new name: the Christian Coalition. This group was unabashedly partisan but disguised its Republican affiliation in order to conform to tax law. The hope of this new, more ecumenical activism was that if Christians proved to be the deciding factor on a majority for the Republican Party, they could change policies on abortion, homosexuality, schools and traditional families as well. In June of 1990, the Christian Coalition paid for a full-page ad in the Washington Post and other national newspapers trying to influence members of congress to vote against funding for the National Endowment for the Arts. The Coalition's plan was to distribute 100,000 reproductions of controversial art by Robert Mapplethorpe and Andres Serrano in districts where members voted for funding. Parts of the ad read as follows:

> "There may be more homosexuals and pedophiles in your district than there are Roman Catholics and Baptists. You may find that the working folks in your district want you to use their tax money to teach their sons how to sodomize each other. You may find that the Roman Catholics in your district want their money spent on pictures of the pope soaked in urine. **BUT MAYBE NOT.**"

By addressing Catholics and Baptists, Robertson clearly tried to widen the spectrum of the Religious Right that was active in politics by making a conscious effort to make the Religious Right more ecumenical.

The first three waves of Right Wing religious movements in the United States were funded and supplied for by the fundamentalist segment of the evangelical community and included anti-communism and education as important topics in their campaigns. The technology of the time was used to reach more and more people although religiously and morally the aim was rather the opposite: to head towards a more homogeneous, less complex time. Nevertheless, secular technology has been welcomed to support this process (Minkenberg 1990: 120).

Each wave eventually died down, because the religious intolerance of the leaders failed to establish a solid grass-roots movement that would last over a longer period of time.

The difference to the Robertson campaign was, however, that for the first time an attempt at a broader variety of Christians was made. During the 1990's the Religious Right extended these efforts by including conservative Jews, Catholics and African Americans. The Christian Coalition initially managed to build a considerable grass-roots movement on a local basis. At one point there were forty county chapters in Virginia, for example, which again were divided into smaller regional chapters. The biggest goal, to have a chapter in every precinct, was never reached; however, these grass-roots organizations did achieve an important presence (Wilcox 2000: 42).

The Religious Right of the 80's worked and campaigned by confronting the public and their counterparts. The Religious Right of the 1990's worked with different tactics. Some Christian Candidates ran as stealth candidates, not admitting their connection to the Religious Right. Not only liberals considered this practice deceptive, their own organizations criticized many stealth candidates for not professing their faith publicly. The Pennsylvania Christian Coalition manual that gave tips on how to run as a stealth candidate was widely distributed and, much to the dismay of the Christian Coalition, reprinted by the media. Eventually the leaders of the organization were forced to come forward with a statement that said that the manual was only a draft produced by an overzealous volunteer.

The current policy of the Religious Right on public speeches, in and running for offices, is to prepare speeches differently for religious and nonreligious audiences. For nonreligious audiences the speeches are supposed to be "mainstreamed" which means that explicit religious language is supposed to be avoided and positions on taxes, crime, abortion and gay rights are to be emphasized. Furthermore, Religious Right candidates have changed their rhetoric towards a "liberal rights" vocabulary. Former rhetoric went along the lines of saying that in a Christian nation such as the United States, public school days should start with a prayer. Now the rhetoric has changed to say that Christian Children have the right to exercise their religious beliefs in saying a prayer. Former arguments that certain textbooks endorsed "evil" lifestyles are being changed. Activists are now arguing that they have a parental right to mold their children's education. Abortion is involving the rights of the unborn. The essential solutions to these issues are the same as in the earlier waves of the Religious Right. The only difference is the justification and the language used.

1.3.5. The Religious Right in the 1990's

The Religious Right of the 1990's and of today has taken up a language of victimization. They are using the same language that they tried to deny to African Americans, women and gays and lesbians in previous years when they claimed to be victims of discrimination. Some Religious Right activists have been copying the efforts of Michael Farris who claimed that being attacked for ties to the Religious Right was having bigotry practiced against him.

The main topics for the Christian Coalition are abortion, education and a group of family/sexuality related issues. While there are positions on more domestic policy related topics such as health care reform, crime, and taxes, the other topics mentioned form the main agenda of the Religious Right. However, the Religious Right of the 1990's consisted of much more transparent political organizations than they used to in previous years. Also their activists can be considered to be more eclectic than their predecessors (Wilcox 2000: 44). These activists are usually involved on a local level dealing with somewhat local issues. The national Religious Right organizations can provide valuable know-how and resources to their local groups which help maintain and recruit new members for the Religious Right.

Both during and after the presidential campaign in 1996, it became evident that the more moderate members of the GOP did not agree with the Christian conservative influence in their party. Candidate Bob Dole did not talk about abortion in his campaign; rather he defended tobacco and attacked milk for being potentially unhealthy. He made clear that he was against "special rights" for gays and lesbians but made even clearer that he was not planning on and never had discriminated on the basis of sexual orientation (Green et al. 1998: 291).

The Religious Right that had formed by the end of the 20th century was a very effective group having learned from the past and having gained experience in the political field. Its efforts became more sophisticated and organized and the recruitment of some adept newcomers to supplement the people who had built the network (Moen 1995: 3) made it more professional.

However, the resignation of the head of the Christian Coalition, Ralph Reed, unsettled the organization and started to stop the progress that the movement had made in the late 20th century. His departure was a destabilizing factor, because his attempt at moderation and at trying to be a mediator between the sometimes rhetorically extreme Pat Robertson and the political landscape was over. His successors, former Reagan cabinet official Donald Hodel and former congressman Randy Tate, were not as successful. The coalition's growth in memberships leveled off as its finances and programs declined (Green 1998). Other factors also contributed to its decline. The longstanding appeal for tax-exempt status was lost in a ruling by the Internal Revenue Service.

The 1996 election results, including the Dole campaign and the lack of attention to social issues by the Republican Congress, contributed to a broader re-assessment of the pragmatic style that Reed and the Coalition had favored. Robertson had to begin to take on a more active role than before and started to show more moderation for some topics. His statements about a change in the program to rather try to limit abortions than to have them banned completely brought resignations on national, state and local levels by people that had been working for the Christian Coalition for years. These people felt betrayed and saw the work that they had been doing as not being valued.

As the efforts to impeach former President Clinton stalled in 1999, the longtime conservative activist member of the Moral Majority, Paul Weyrich, declared the culture war as lost and advised conservative Christians to begin creating an alternative culture and to withdraw from mainstream culture. Cal Thomas and Ed Dobson who are former Moral Majority activists claimed in their book "Blinded by Might" that the true mission of evangelicals was to save souls rather than to be seduced by the lure of political power.

However, some other elements of the movement did experience growth, especially those that were loosely connected to Focus on the Family such as the Family Research Council (FRC) and the Campaign for Working Families (CWF). Their heads, Gary Bauer and James Dobson, were now rivaling Pat Robertson and the Christian Coalition.

Some of the movement's resources joined other parts of the GOP. Ralph Reed became a campaign consultant, some of the activists became members of the Federation of Republican assemblies (a conservative state-level GOP faction) and Gary Bauer planned on running in the 2000 Republican presidential campaign. Some even went on to minor parties such as Howard Phillips' U.S. Taxpayers Party. Pat Buchanan ran as an independent presidential candidate.

The Religious Right as a whole is currently not as strong as it was at the end of the 1980's. However, as I will show in the following chapters, it is still a force that has certain strengths. These strengths are capable of influencing the political system and public policy.

2. Structures and Political Influence of the Religious Right

2.1 Organizations of the Religious Right

This table is designed to give you an overview of the most important and well accomplished organizations of the Religious Right. Much of the information presented is taken from the website of People for the American Way www.pfaw.org. This site is an excellent source for information on other right wing organizations as well.

Name of Organization	Headed by	Founded in	Finances	Impact	Goals and Issues
National Right to Life Committee www.nrlc.org	President Wanda Franz	1973	$12.4 million (1998 revenue)	3,000+ state chapters in all 50 states and D.C	The passage of a constitutional amendment banning all abortion, partial-birth abortion, euthanasia, stem cell research, and in vitro fertilization. Opposes RU-486 and some forms of contraceptives including the "Pill".
Heritage Foundation www.heritage.org	Executive Director Dr. Edwin Feulner	1973 by Joseph Coors (of Coors Beer) and Paul Weyrich	$38 million annual budget in 2000, $197 million overall assets, 205 employees	200,000 members nationwide, takes credit for most of George W. Bush's policies.	Mission: "To formulate and promote conservative public policies based on the principles of free enterprise, limited government, individual freedom, traditional American Values and a strong national defense".

Focus on the Family www.family.org	Dr. James C. Dobson	1977 by Dobson	$128.9 million budget in 2000 approximately 1,300 employees	36 state chapters, largest international religious-right group in the United States, multi media empire with its own zip code, campus and over ten publications	FOF is anti-choice, anti-gay, anti-multicultural, and against sex education curricula that are not strictly abstinence only. They provide Christian "self help" material in order to address these issues.
Family Research Council www.frc.org	Kenneth L. Connor	1983	$10 million (2000 revenue), 120 employees	40 state groups, affiliated with Dobson's Focus on the Family, formerly headed by Dobson's long-time protégée Gary Bauer, is seen as Focus' political arm in Washington	Since the early 1990's FRC has been pushing "traditional family values" by lobbying for state-sponsored prayer in public schools, private school vouchers, abstinence-only programs, filtering software on public library computers and the right to discriminate against gay men and lesbian women. It's also working against public funding of the National Endowment for the Arts and the Corporation for Public Broadcasting. It would like to "disestablish" the Department of Education.

Eagle Forum www.eagleforum.org	Phyllis Schlafly	1972	$2.3 (2000 budget), 8 employees	30 chapters listed on website, Schlafly takes credit for defeating the Equal Rights Amendment, and her anti-feminism efforts made her a household name in the Equal Rights amendment battle in the 1970's. She was responsible for popularizing the misconception that if the ERA was passed, separate bathrooms for the sexes would be illegal.	The eagles forum was created in order to combat the ERA; however, it has over time evolved to a group battling reproductive rights, AIDS education, sexual harassment legislation, federal support for daycare and family leave, United States involvement with the United Nations, the international Chemical Weapons Treaty, affirmative action, bilingual education, multiculturalism and diversity education, gay and lesbian rights, teaching the theory of evolution in schools, pornography, and immigration.

Name of Organization	Headed by	Founded in	Finances	Impact	Goals and Issues
Concerned Women for America www.cwa.org	Beverly LaHaye/ Sandy Rios	1979	$12.7 million (2000 budget), 34 employees	Claims over 500,000 members in 500 regional groups across the country	It is the largest public policy women's organization. It wants to protect "traditional family values" that support the Biblical design of the family. CWA identifies feminism as "anti-god, anti-family". It has lobbied against the Freedom of Choice Act, as well as against gay rights in many states. One of the newer issues is lobbying against the Harry Potter books, arguing that it promotes witchcraft.
Christian Coalition www.cc.org	Roberta Combs, formerly headed by Pat Robertson	1989	Contributions dropped from a record of $26.5 million in 1996 to approximately $3 million in 2000	Claims nearly 2 million members, according to People for the American Way is more likely. 30 chapters across the U.S. 300,000 – 400,000 members	Control agenda of Republican party by working from the grass-roots up, and train and educat their own candidates in order to elect them into public office. Claim to having distributed 70 million voter guides in the 2000 presidential election.

2.2. Organizational Structures of the Religious Right

When looking at how the Religious Right organizes itself, it is important to note that despite the heterogeneous nature of it, there are quite a few very strong organizations within it. These institutionalized factions of the Religious Right have a tendency to lean towards Christian nationalism which is rooted in the Calvinistic tradition of settlers in the Massachusetts Puritan Colonies where dissidents were banished as heretics. Some of these organizations are openly politically active, such as the Christian Coalition, others are insisting that they are purely ministry organizations, such as Focus on the Family. I will describe some of these organizations on the following pages, because I believe that they are a crucial factor to the success that the Religious Right had in the 2000 campaign. The institutionalized branch of the Religious Right can be described as decentralized and factioned. They are generally well funded although in recent years public financial support for some of them, such as the Christian Coalition and the Promise Keepers, has declined. Others, such as Focus on the Family, are thriving. One cannot underestimate the strength the movement gains from its grass-roots efforts. And while, generally, these organizations have come a long way from being pure grass-roots organizations and have undergone a tremendous professionalization, their grass-roots activities present a core element of their overall approach.

2.2.1. The Christian Coalition

The Christian Coalition was founded by Pat Robertson on September 25, 1989 in Atlanta. At the first organizational meeting, Robertson introduced Ralph Reed[57] as "the first staff member of a group that as yet had no name, a development that surprised me as much as everyone else" (Reed 1994: 1-3). According to Reed, the actual mission for the majority of attending people was to create an "American Congress of Christian Citizens" rather than to create a grass-root organization. At first Reed and Robertson aimed for a compromise by allowing those dual missions. However, by March 1990 grass-root organizing had become the sole purpose of the organization.

Reed describes in his book "Politically Incorrect" how the Christian Coalition started out in a warehouse with the remains of Robertson's presidential campaign spread out around them. The new organization

---

[57] For more on Reed and Robertson see Chapter 4.3.

benefited strongly from the lists of donors and volunteers that they could call upon to build a new organization. In addition, the Republican Senatorial Committee gave a one-time contribution of $64,000 which made a big difference to the start of the Christian Coalition.

The mission of the Christian Coalition is summarized in the following five-fold statement:

Our Five - Fold Mission

Represent the pro-family point of view before local councils, schoolboards, state legislatures and Congress.

Speak out in the public arena and in the media.

Train leaders for effective social and political action.

Inform pro-family voters about timely issues and legislation.

Protest anti-Christianity bigotry and defend the rights of people of faith.

In the beginning, the Christian Coalition applied for the tax-exempt status of a nonprofit organization under IRS code 501(c)(w). After a ten year long battle, the IRS finally declared the Christian Coalition as non eligible for tax exempt status in June of 1999. It will have to pay back taxes for the past ten years. However, donors have not been able to write off donations which means that there is quite a wide area of possibilities to choose from when it comes to taking action. Some of the possibilities include lobbying public officials, producing voter guides, or engaging in voter education. However, they officially cannot be partisan and on much of their direct mail literature say that they're not. After the rejection of the tax exempt status, the Coalition announced it would reorganize in order to reapply for the tax exempt status. Robertson served as the president while Reed, until his departure, served as the executive director. The Christian Coalition is structured as a network of state affiliates and local chapters. Every chapter has to gain its own tax exempt status from the IRS and obtain a charter from the Board of Directors of the national Christian Coalition. Individual chapters do not receive financial help from the national organization and are a separate legal entity (Watson 1999: 53). Any state affiliate that does not comply with the exact rules of the national headquarter can be cut off due to the fact that the charters have to be renewed annually.

In 1996 donations to the Christian Coalition rose to an all time high of $26.5 million, however, in 2002 donations dropped to an estimated $3 million. Around 1996 there were three major publications by the Christian Coalition. The most important one was "Christian American" which started out in 1990 as a quarterly four-page newsletter. As early as 1991 it had changed its format into a thirty-two page tabloid. It contained "Pat's View" which was a question and answer column by Pat Robertson. In September 1995, the magazine was published 6 times a year in a 34 page format and was becoming less aggressive. However, as donations started to decrease, the publication of "Christian American" was given up. When Pat Robertson left the Christian Coalition, he took "Pat's View" and changed it into "Pat's Perspective" which features the same question and answer style but is only available via his personal homepage www.patrobertson.com.

Many of the publications of the nineties are now only available via the internet. However, the Christian Coalition is still distributing printed score cards for political candidates. In the 2000 presidential campaign the Christian Coalition claims that it sent out 70 million voter guides to members and conservative churches in all states which is the largest campaign it has ever undertaken. Wilcox (2002: 116) judges this figure as "undoubtedly exaggerated".

After Robertson's departure in 2001, their lobbying office in Washington D.C. became the new "national headquarters" although most of the mailing equipment and staff are still situated in Virginia. The Washington D.C. office was opened in 1993. Its purpose was to monitor legislation and federal agencies and to lobby members of congress and have an access to national media.

In addition to efforts involving technology, the Christian Coalition holds training sessions on both a national and local level. Its aim is to provide activists with know-how for putting what the Christian Coalition leadership has decided upon into action.

The national training conferences are titled "Road to Victory" and concentrate on speeches and workshops. The speeches are given by conservative politicians on various issues concerning abortion, homosexuality, and school prayer. The workshops have a more practical approach with instructions on for how to lobby your legislator for example. During the national conferences, other groups and organizations of the Religious Right will typically set up information booths and display tables to lobby for their own cause (Watson 1999: 57). At the 2000 "Road to

Victory" conference, speakers included: Former Senate Majority Leader Trent Lott, House Majority Leader Dick Armey, House Speaker Dennis Hastert, Majority Whip Tom DeLay, Rev. Jerry Falwell, RNC Chairman Jim Nicholson, and the then-presidential candidate George W. Bush via videotape.

On the local level, the Christian Coalition holds one and two day seminars across the nation. In these seminars, which have a very hands-on approach, attendees are taught about grass-roots political activism. Identifying "pro-family voters" is another goal which includes having names referred from other Christian Coalition activists, church membership lists or lists of people that have signed certain petitions. Door-to-door calls are a common instrument in approaching people whose views are unknown.

So called "church-liaisons" are another way to keep close ties to the community. Church liaisons are simply members of the Christian Coalition that take their cause to their local church. One of the main goals is to conduct voter registration drives. Considering that the majority of Christian Coalition members attend churches that can be found in the conservative / evangelical category, these voter registrations mainly strengthen the religious conservative block of voters (Watson 1999: 58).

Another main goal for the church-liaisons is the distribution of voter guides which are published by the Christian Coalition. These voter guides compare candidates based on their past voting behavior. The issues are selected so that the conservative Republican candidate looks most favorable. However, at times the Christian Coalition uses manipulative language to point out certain candidates. For example, one candidate was labeled as a proponent for "tax-funded obscene art" because he was a supporter of the National Endowment of the Arts (People for the American Way Webpage). These guides are mainly distributed on the last Sunday before elections in order to prevent candidates from taking action if they feel they have been represented unfairly.

On July 30, 1996, the Federal Election Commission (FEC) filed a lawsuit against the Christian Coalition for distributing partisan voter guides in the 1990 and 1992 elections and for coordinating their activities with the Bush reelection campaign in 1992. In the end, this charge cost the Christian Coalition its attempted tax exempt status.

In the beginning, the major tactics for gaining influence were concentrated on the local level. They consisted of targeting low-profile local elections for school boards or hospital boards, for example. Churches in these areas were targeted with a "get-out-the-votes" principle which included instructions and training for Christian Coalition candidates on how to hide their actual views from the public. Ralph Reed told some members at a 1992 meeting "The first strategy, and in many ways the most important strategy, for evangelicals is secrecy" (PFAW-Christian Coalition page). This strategy became very successful when, in a 1990 race in San Diego, CA, the Christian Coalition won 60 out of 90 seats for local offices.

The Coalition, under intense pressure for its stealth tactics, has since changed its approach. Today's church-liaisons, for example, are expected to obtain their church leadership's permission for voter education activities. There is a structured "how to" guide in Christian Coalition manuals that advises activists to start "Civic Concerns Ministries" (Watson 1999: 59). By starting these ministries within a church, pastors can stay outside of them; however, existing church groups, the parallel to the local chapters, are providing a receptive ground for recruiting volunteers or activists. While most of the chairmen of the Moral Majority of the 80's were clergy, only few of the Christian Coalition's leaders are.

In recent years, the Christian Coalition has faced some serious set-backs. Besides the rejection of the tax exempt status, its very successful leader, Ralph Reed, left the organization in order to form his own political consulting firm.

The Christian Coalition had to seriously cut back on staff due to the decline of donations which, especially in times of a conservative religious President, are hard to come by. As soon as President Clinton left office, one of the Christian Coalition's main justifications for its work and, thus, for the need of donations, vanished. Accordingly, the $26.5 million of donations in 1996 dwindled to an estimated $3 million in the year 2000 (PFAW homepage). As a result, minority outreach programs were cancelled.

In 1999, Robertson was pressured into leaving the board of Laura Ashley Holdings' PLC after gay activists accused him of being homophobic and were planning protests. The Bank of Scotland refused to sign a contract with Robertson Financial Services after Robertson's comments about Scotland being a "dark land" in which homosexuals receive disproportional access to power (Edsall et al 1999: A04). Furthermore, ten black employees filed a lawsuit against the Christian Coalition for being treated in a highly segregated way in 2001. Black employees were being spied on and had to eat their lunches at their desks as opposed to the white employees who had access to a lunch / kitchen area. The new executive director Roberta Combs allegedly told African American employees to enter the building through the back door (Weekend Edition - Sunday (NPR), 03-31-2001).

Robertson left the Christian Coalition in 2001; he is now concentrating his work on the Christian Broadcasting Network (CBN). In 2002 the Christian Coalition was facing a serious decline in donations and was struggling to stay relevant.

2.2.2. Focus On the Family

Focus on the Family was founded in 1977 and is still headed by its founder Dr. James Dobson. It is operating internationally and is the largest organization of the Religious Right in the United States. According to www.ministrywatch.com, in the year 2000, Focus' annual budget consisted of $128.8 million dollars, and in 2002 they had $126.2 million dollars. At the moment, the staff consists of about 1300 employees, and about 2.3 million people are subscribing to various Focus magazines which cover an area from general family issues to teen magazines to political/cultural magazines. Its radio broadcasts are carried by approximately 3000 stations in the United States and are listened to by an estimated 200 million people (www.ministrywatch.com). Worldwide, the Focus broadcasts can be listened to in 98 countries and in 9 different languages. Dobson's program, interestingly, is carried by a state-owned radio station in China.

The mission statement of Focus on the Family says that their goal is "To cooperate with the Holy Spirit in disseminating the Gospel of Jesus Christ to as many people as possible, and, specifically, to accomplish that objective by helping to preserve traditional values and the institution of the family" (www.family.org).

After starting out in 1977 with a half hour radio program which aired weekly and after becoming increasingly popular and lucrative in 1978, Dobson left his job at the USC[58] in order to start the "not-for-profit" Focus on the Family. Radio ministry grew stronger and stronger over the next two decades and became the most important part of Focus on the Family. They have a daily half hour program and a ninety seconds commentary that is being aired on many secular radio stations (Diamond 1998: 31). In addition, the main magazine "Focus on the Family" is being sent out to about 2

---

[58] University of Southern California

million listeners. It features answers to down to earth problems or tasks such as how to prepare children for a hospital stay. Another big topic is infertility. Although childlessness is undoubtedly a disappointment for those who wish to have children, the magazine portrays childlessness as the ultimate tragedy in life. It also portrays the traditional family, including a male breadwinner and a stay-at-home-mom, as the best possible solution. Children and parents are encouraged to play traditional roles and are thus being prepared to reinforce the traditional family on a political level as well.

The political magazine "Citizen", with tips on activism and suggestions for voter drives and the like, goes out to about 130,000 listeners. Its topics concentrate on "family values" and are anti-gay, anti-affirmative action and strictly anti-abortion[59].

Also, Dobson sends out a monthly newsletter to everyone on his mailing list in which he gives his view on certain political or cultural issues. Again, the main issues concentrate on "family values" reflecting a strictly traditional view.

About $4 million of the Focus budget goes to a "public policy" category every year which includes lobbying and voter education. Green (2000: 7) mentions that one of the few organizations of the Religious Right that actually experienced growth in the second half of the 1990's was Focus on the Family. The political influence Focus on the Family was executing in the 1998 elections, according to Green (ibid.), rivaled that of Pat Robertson and the Christian Coalition.

Focus on the Family also provides an answering service for listeners that send in letters with their questions. The staff is trained to look for emergency cases such as people that are likely to commit suicide who are then contacted directly. They are referred to counselors who are trained professionals to deal with their cases. The other letters are being answered by staffers that use generic paragraphs that Dobson has written in advance; in addition, they send information on books that are dealing with the same topics. People's emotional needs are being met through these letters which makes it appear like somebody is taking their problems and issues seriously. This factor alone makes these people more likely to listen to Dobson when

---

[59] A favorite topic includes testimonies from women who have gotten pregnant through rape who have decided to carry out their pregnancies. Questionable studies then "show" that women who have conceived through rape can cope better if they do not have abortions.

he gives advice in the political area as well. He appears to be the one "moral instance" that does not change and that they can rely on.

His potential for influencing his constituents is tremendous.

The goal of Focus on the Family to influence national politics became particularly clear in a 1989 outline that Dobson wrote. According to him, in 1988 a million calls and letters had been reaching Congress that were launched by the radio program. The two issues[60] that Focus was lobbying against passed; furthermore, Dobson used this experience to start a four part program to make Focus more effective in Washington.

The first step involved merging Focus with the Family Research Council which was headed by Gary Bauer. Bauer was portrayed to listeners as the man that was lobbying for conservative Christians in Washington. His ties, dating back to his involvement with the Reagan administrations, were to ensure that the voice of Focus was being heard on Capitol Hill.

The second step was confined to the state level and included the formation of think tanks that would help lobby the state legislatures.

Step three was aimed at the Citizen magazine. In addition to the national issues that it was reporting on, it was also equipped monthly with a four page inlet that made readers aware of what was going on in their home state. This inlet made it easier for readers to lobby close to home on issues that they felt involved their immediate surroundings.

The last and fourth step involved the radio program which started broadcasting a new segment called "Family News in Focus" which featured political news that Dobson considered relevant for his Christian listeners.

Diamond researched the local seminars from Focus on the Family (1998: 34). She found that they are organized by the state think tanks and local churches. Materials come from Colorado Springs, the organization's headquarters in Colorado. She finds it quite different from the very practical approach that the Christian Coalition takes at local seminars. "It was like Focus assumed its listeners were still amateurs and even gun-shy about politics" (ibid). Speakers emphasized the importance of the "love thy neighbor" message rather than to act out of fear, anger or hatred in order to

---

[60] The one issue was the nomination of Robert Bork to the Supreme Court, and the second issue was the expansion of a federal rights bill that was aimed at expanding protection for disabled people as well as minorities.

win souls and evangelize. Another motivation should be the biblical demand for being a good citizen on an individual level. Secular society should not be feared, but by entering political institutions, Christians could make their voices be heard. There were no direct strategies for voter registration or lobbying; There was just general encouragement in order to become involved. However, Diamond writes that the practical instructions were given in subsequent seminars held by the state think tanks. The participants for the state seminars were selected by the think tank members, because they felt they were the best judges for who would become an effective activist.

Focus on the Family also helps the state think tanks in producing 60 second radio spots that are being aired on local radio stations that provide free air time. These spots are particularly helpful for those activists that neither have the skills nor the technical equipment to produce them.

In Colorado, Focus helped the organization "Colorado for Family Values" in the preparation and lobbying of support for the 2nd Amendment ballot initiative. Until Focus broadcasted a nationwide program on it, the initiative had not been particularly successful. Afterwards, however, the situation changed as Kevin Tebedo, the CFV organizer says. People started calling in order to massively help the organization. After this initial success, Focus helped CFV produce radio spots that would then be distributed to local radio stations. As mentioned earlier, the 2nd Amendment passed; however, it was later overruled by the Supreme Court.

In February of 1998, Dobson gave a warning shot at a meeting of a conservative organization "Council for National Policy". The member list reads like the "Who is Who" in social conservative politics. Dobson gave a speech that outlined how the GOP has abandoned its evangelical voters.

> "Does the Republican Party want our votes, no strings attached--to court us every two years, and then to say, 'Don't call me; I'll call you'--and to not care about the moral law of the universe?...Is that what they want? Is that the way the system works? Is this the way it's going to be? If it is, I'm gone, and if I go, I will do everything I can to take as many people with me as possible" (Statement from 2/7/98 Council for National Policy meeting, Wash. Times 2/17/98).

He added that he was considering temporarily leaving Focus on the Family in order to become more directly involved in political action without endangering Focus' tax exempt status.

The GOP promptly responded. Never before had so many "pro family" votes been on the agenda (Carney 1998).

2.2.3. The National Right to Life Committee

The National Right to Life Committee was founded in 1973 as an answer to the Supreme Court Ruling of Roe vs. Wade. It is headed by Wanda Franz who is a Professor of Developmental Psychology at West Virginia University. It is affiliated with the National Right to Life Committee Educational Trust Fund, National Right to Life Conventions, National Right to Life political action committee and the Horatio R. Storer Foundation[61].

The Committee is a very influential organization and the largest anti-abortion organization in the United States. The 1998 revenue was $12.4 million, and the 2001 revenue was $15 million. It claims to have "nearly 400,000 subscribers" on its "Hot List" which is an e-mail news service on pressing issues and action alerts. In addition, the National Right to Life Committee has a monthly newsletter that it sends out to approximately the same amount of people.

The NRLC is a grass-roots organization and specializes in lobbying congress. It organizes grass-roots activities directed at anti-abortion issues. It is mainly working for an amendment that bans all abortions; however, they are also involved in issues concerning human cloning and euthanasia. The NRLC opposes RU-486 and some forms of contraceptives including the pill. In addition, they are speaking out against the Equal Rights Amendment (ERA).

In the 2000 election, the NRLC PAC spent $2.7 million on the campaign for George W. Bush[62]. The NRLC PAC also contributed to other pro-life Republican candidates to gain seats in the Senate: $205,896 for Senator

---

[61] Horatio R. Storer (1830-1922) was a physician who was against abortion and who basically founded the American anti-abortion movement in the 1800's.

[62] All numbers are taken from an article called "Republican Party Donates to Right to Life" by Cynthia L. Cooper which can be found at http://www.womensenews.org/article.cfm?aid=1259.

John Cornyn of Texas; 192,241 for Senator James Talent of Missouri; $126,899 for Senator Saxby Chambliss of Georgia; $122,051 for Senator Wayne Allard of Colorado; and $105,227 for Senator Elizabeth Dole. All of these Senators have been consistently voting anti-abortion or anti-partial-birth-abortion[63].

By law, non-profit organizations that influence elections by donating money are required to file reports on who they are giving to. The NRLC registered to be such an organization after the law had been passed in 2000[64], but they have never filed any donation reports. The committee is actively trying to hide where its contributions are going. It is challenging campaign reform laws throughout the country and is now fighting reforms that will require disclosure of the hidden funders of election attack ads in the federal court. It would appear that they don't want their donations to be publicized.

According to Deborah Goldberg of the Democracy Program of the Brennan Center for Justice in New York City, litigation papers and other documents show the connection between the National Right to Life Committee and the pro-life wing of the Republican Party. If the campaign reform laws passed, the connection between the two could be even more revealed than now. Goldberg claims that "[w]e know that the Republican Party gives money to the right-to-life groups" (Cooper 2003). And there is another indicator that supports this claim:

The "Better Business Bureau Wise Giving Alliance" states that the Republican Party and related committees are making substantial contributions. In an affidavit that was filed with the federal court by the NRLC in October 2002, executive director David N. O'Steen stated that the committee "has received donations from political parties or committees". 98% of the politicians that the NRLC supported were Republicans which means that even though O'Steen did not explicitly state that the political parties he referred to were Republican, the probability is very high.

In this mutual working alliance, members of the Republican Party have also signed fund-raising letters for the NRLC. According to Cooper, the Republican Congressional Representative of Illinois, Henry Hyde, has received contributions from the National Right to Life Political Action Committee which is also run by O'Steen. In return, Hyde signed fundraising

---

[63] The emotionally connotated term "partial-birth-abortion" was initially introduced by the NRLC in order to replace the more neutral term "late-term-abortion (Cooper 2003).

[64] Groups are supposed to register under the "Section 527 groups" with the IRS.

Second Chapter: Organizational Structures of the Religious Right

letters for the NRLC in 1997 and 1998 and was simultaneously one of the major forces behind the impeachment of then Democratic President, Bill Clinton.

According to a 1998 congressional report[65] by the Senate Governmental Affairs Committee on campaign money, the NRLC received approximately $650,000 in 1996 from the Republican National Committee. It is a major player which partly draws its strength from its close connections with the Republican Party. It calls itself non-partisan to cover up for the fact that it is very closely affiliated with one major party.

2.2.4. Concerned Women for America

Concerned Women for America was founded in 1979 by Beverly LaHaye, wife of fundamentalist Southern Baptist preacher, Tim LaHaye. In 2000, CWA's annual budget consisted of $12.7 million-a number that seems to be quite stable throughout the years. CWA claims to have about 500,000 members who are divided up into 500 regional groups around the country. Its staff consists of 25 employees.

CWA[66] has two major publications: *Family Voice* is published monthly and has about 200,000 subscribers, and *Family Watch* is a church communication magazine and reaches approximately 500,000 readers every month. In addition, CWA offers several books, audio-tapes and video tapes on various issues. They can be purchased via their website and in selected Christian book-stores. CWA has a daily radio show which is aired on 75 stations and which, according to People for the American Way, reaches about 1 million listeners every week.

Affiliated groups are: Concerned Women for America Education and Legal Defense Foundation, Concerned Women for America Legislative Action committee (CWALAC), the Beverly LaHaye Institute and the Culture and Family Institute.

---

[65] Senate Governmental Affairs Committee: 1998 Congressional Report On Campaign Money.
[66] Concerned Women for America works closely with Phillys Schlaffly's Eagle Forum which is another Religious Right organization targeted at women. It has approximately 80,000 members and credits itself with defeating the Equal Rights Amendment.

CWA is the largest Religious Right organization that is targeted at women. It also claims to be the largest women's organization in the United States.

Beverly LaHaye claims in her own words that she founded the organization because she felt that women like her were underrepresented in the media. She claims that one night she was watching popular feminist, Betty Friedan, on TV who apparently was claiming that her views were shared by a large group of other American women. LaHaye then decided that her own views were shared by many women as well, if not more, and in 1978 founded an organization that was to combat the American feminist movement.

According to this excerpt of Beverly LaHaye's writings, Minkenberg's (1990) theory of a "counter-counter movement" as one of the major forces behind the advancement of the Religious Right is verified. Feminism is seen as a threat to the American mainstream culture. It is perceived as the reason for the high divorce rate in the United States and for many of the social problems in general. In reaction to this point of view, feminism must be combated so women can return to their God-given roles as submissive wives.

As LaHaye writes in her book "The Spirit Controlled Woman", proper women are "truly liberated because they are totally submissive to their husbands" (1976: 71). On feminism she states: "Most women know the feminist agenda has failed. They see our culture crumbling from its influence. In fact, feminism has harmed women and families worldwide as its proponents have used the United Nations to spread their agenda" (http://www.cwfa.org/library/_familyvoice/1999-07/4-5.shtml).

CWA is divided into two parts - at least when it comes to tax purposes. Concerned Women for America Education and Legal Defense Foundation is a charitable organization confined to non-partisan, non-political grass-roots lobbying under federal income-tax exempt 501 (c) 3 while Concerned Women for America, Inc., is a non-partisan lobbying group that can act in favor or opposition to a certain bill or ballot measure under 501 (c) 4. The major difference between the two is that donations to 501 (c) 3 are tax deductible while donations to 501 (c) 4 are not.

The CWA headquarter is located in Washington D.C. and has 25 staff members. Generally speaking, the headquarter controls CWA's philosophical direction; however, each local chapter has some freedom when it comes to addressing local issues. Other than that, specific instructions are given to local chapters on how to deal with issues that are of national importance.

CWA presents itself as anti-gay, anti-choice, anti-feminism and anti sex-education and is trying to promote what they call the "biblical structure of the family". Their own structure of the local chapter is based on the biblical number of seven, mixed with a phenomenon that is especially popular with fundamentalist/evangelical circles: The so called prayer chain group. It consists of seven members and is headed by one prayer leader; seven such groups then form a prayer chain. Seven of those chains constitute a local chapter of CWA which is then headed by a chapter leader. In the end every chapter contains fifty members. They are being coordinated by a regional leader who reports to the national headquarters in Washington D.C.

This strategy is also applied to lobbying and getting out phone calls to people that can shower representatives with letters. This strategy is being described at length in a pamphlet called "The Kitchen Table Activist" published by the CWA headquarters in the early years of the Reagan administration.

Generally, action directives are called "special messages" and are being sent by President LaHaye. She then activates the so called "535 Program" which refers to 435 Representatives and 100 Senators. Thousands of letters and phone calls usually result from this program, and representatives are being substantially pressured to vote the "right" way. They know that one "wrong" vote will not be forgotten and will become an issue at the next election when scorecards are being issued again. Although some of the representatives might not necessarily agree on the standpoints of CWA, they try not to become a target of this, or any other, organization of the Religious Right in the next elections. It is often easier, despite one's own opinion or beliefs, to vote with the majority of activists rather than with the majority of voters in order to be "safe" from their attacks (Wilcox 2000).

Beverly LaHaye clearly says that she thinks that religion should play a major part in politics. In Ms. Magazine she stated: "Yes, religion and politics do mix. America is a nation based on biblical principles. Christian values dominate our government. The test of those values is the Bible. Politicians who do not use the Bible to guide their public and private lives do not belong in office" (Feb. 1987).

During the Ashcroft confirmation hearings in the Senate, the CWA, among other "pro-family" (as if the majority of their opponents would be anti-family) organizations, held a press conference which aimed at mobilizing activists. Their goal was to support Ashcroft and resulted in, as they claim, 13,000 e-mails, phone calls and hand-delivered information to senators. The CWA called the opponents of Ashcroft "anti-religionists".

The CWA covers a wide array of issues. For example, the CWA has been very active in fighting Harry Potter books. It has published videos such as "Harry Potter: Witchcraft Repackaged: Making Evil Look Innocent"[67], or books such as "Harry Potter: Seduction of the Occult" which state that these books are promoting the practice of witchcraft among children.

CWA is promoting and providing material on teaching Creationism and the "Intelligent Design Theory"[68] in the classroom. On the same hand, CWA is promoting the de-funding of the National Endowment for the Arts (NEA) by having Beverly LaHaye testify before the Committee on Appropriations, the Interior Subcommittee of the House of Representatives.

CWA's anti-gay programs include work on many issues. Some examples are a strong support of the Boy Scout's ban on gay participants, an opposition to any openly gay members of the Bush administration and a disapproval of all gay and lesbian civil rights measures. They are also supporting the right to discriminate against gay and lesbians in employment. CWA is also an avid supporter of the "Truth in Love" campaign which promotes that homosexuality is a sin and that homosexuals can be "healed" from homosexuality by turning to Christ and relying on the Bible. Beverly LaHaye has been warning her constituents about homosexuals for years: "[They] want their depraved 'values' to become our children's values. Homosexuals expect society to embrace their immoral way of life. Worse yet, they are looking for new recruits!" (CWA direct mail, 5/92).

Tim and Beverly LaHaye have given Jerry Falwell's Liberty University, where Beverly LaHaye is a trustee, 4.5 million dollars in 2001.

The CWA is also active legally. They filed a suit on behalf of an anti abortion protester who was trying to hinder people from entering an abortion clinic despite the federal Freedom of Access to Clinic Entrances Act (FACE) which banned protesters from blocking clinic entrances.

---

[67] Published by Tim LaHaye, Beverly LaHaye's husband.

[68] "Intelligent Design Theory" is a new aim at Creationism. Rather than explaining that all life on earth has been created by God, it claims that all biochemical processes were designed rather than coming to life arbitrarily.

Second Chapter: Organizational Structures of the Religious Right

2.2.5. The Promise Keepers

The Promise Keepers (PK) were founded on March 20, 1990, by University of Colorado Football Coach, Bill McCartney, and his friend Dave Wardell. They felt it was time for a Christ centered organization for men that would help them to become more involved with Jesus. This involvement was supposed to be transformed into turning their lives around and focusing more attention on their families. According to McCartney it was important to build such an organization for men because similar organizations already existed for women.

Their idea was to gather men in order to pray and to worship God. There were two approaches:

- Gather men at the grass-roots level in their hometowns for a weekly meeting of small groups with other men. These meetings were shepherded by leaders which also served as some kind of outlet for confessions. The objective was for participants to read the Bible, to pray and worship God, and to confess sins about actions somehow detrimental to their marriages or families. Through the showing of repentance and the promise of improvement their family lives were supposed to make a turn for the better.

- Gather men once a year at the so called "Promise Keeper Rallies" which were held at stadiums across the entire USA. During their high times in the middle nineties, these events would attract over a million men in 22 stadiums. These "men only" events would sometimes be prepared by wives and other volunteers who would anoint every seat in the stadium and, therefore, bless it the day before the actual rally. These rallies would appeal to the audience by evoking feelings of being part of a large mass praying, singing, chanting and worshipping God. Speakers would give lectures and musicians would lead the singing. Men could come up to the front and receive blessings for being "revived".

The Promise Keepers are being held accountable for the "Seven Promises" that being a Promise Keeper is all about.

1. A Promise Keeper is committed to honoring Jesus Christ through worship, prayer and obedience to God's Word in the power of the Holy Spirit.

2. A Promise Keeper is committed to pursuing vital relationships with a few other men, understanding that he needs brothers to help him keep his promises.

3. A Promise Keeper is committed to practicing spiritual, moral, ethical and sexual purity.

4. A Promise Keeper is committed to building strong marriages and families through love, protection and biblical values.

5. A Promise Keeper is committed to supporting the mission of his church by honoring and praying for his pastor and by actively giving his time and resources.

6. A Promise Keeper is committed to reaching beyond any racial and denominational barriers to demonstrate the power of biblical unity.

7. A Promise Keeper is committed to influencing his world, being obedient to the Great Commandment[69] (see Mark 12:30-31) and the Great Commission[70] (see Matthew 28:19-20).

The Promise Keepers claim to be a group that is non-political. However, actions taken by the Promise Keepers and connections to Religious Right organizations make that claim seem invalid. As early as 1992, the Promise Keepers received $10,000 from James Dobson. He has also been a guest speaker several times along with Pat Robertson and other political figures of the Religious Right. Also, at the October 4th "March on Washington Rally"

---

[69] Mark 12:30-31: Love the Lord your God with all your heart and with all your soul and with all your mind and with all your strength. The second is this: Love your neighbor as yourself. (NIV)

[70] Matthew 28:19-20: Therefore go and make disciples of all nations, baptizing them in the name of the Father and of the Son and of the Holy Spirit, and teaching them to obey everything I have commanded you. And surely I am with you always, to the very end of the age. (NIV)

that was held in 1997, Promise Keepers officials were receiving massive personal support by leaders of the politically established Religious Right community of Washington D.C. In a Larry King interview right after the rally, PK leader McCartney praised James Dobson of Focus on the Family who had helped the Promise Keepers out financially (www.cdsresearch.org/pkwatch2/supp6.htm). In addition, Gary Bauer's Family Research Council, which is the political arm of Focus on the Family, placed signs welcoming the Promise Keepers all over the city. Promise Keepers have close contact to other leaders of the Religious Right:

- Pat Robertson has had McCartney as a guest on his TV show "The 700 Club" many times and has also said on his program that the Promise Keepers represent a major part of "God's plan for America".

- Not only has James Dobson provided considerable financial help to the beginning of the Promise Keepers, he also promotes the organization on his radio program and published their official program "Seven Promises of a Promise Keeper" in 1984.

- Bauer, who ran for President in the 2000 elections, has been a speaker at Promise Keepers events where he made it clear that, in his opinion, there is a need to elect "Godly men" to public office. The organization that Bauer headed before his run for president was the Family Research Council which is a political spin-off of Focus on the Family.

- Bill Bright, whose organization centers on prayer at public schools and universities, has provided the Promise Keepers with volunteers and material support.

- Charles Colson, who is the founder of Prison Fellowships and who was convicted in the Watergate scandal promoted a GOP gubernatorial candidate in North Carolina at a Promise Keepers event in 1996.

- Jerry Falwell has spoken at Promise Keepers events. Although he no longer heads the Moral Majority, he is still active in the political realm.

Dr. James Kennedy is a Religious Right organizer and father of the "Reclaiming America"[71] Conferences.

---

[71] "The Center for Reclaiming America"'s goal is to train people to work politically in their communities. It features a Bible centered political agenda in which it tries to further right-wing causes.

PK founder McCartney was part of the Colorado for Family Values group that was the initiator behind the Amendment 2 initiative which actually passed to become Colorado State law. However, it was later ruled unconstitutional by the Supreme Court[72]. McCartney has called homosexuals an "abomination".

PK Leader Raleigh Washington has been quoted saying:

"There is no way this group can restrict itself when it comes to public policy. We are producing leaders in this organization. They will enter the political sphere" (http://now.org/issues/right/promise/mythfact.html)

McCartney himself has been criticized for using his publicly funded position in order to make pre-game prayers mandatory. He is a member of the WOG (Word of God) community which was described in the National Catholic Reporter as a cult-like organization which practices "shepherding / discipleship". In its structure of authority, members confess sins and submit their lives to a "shepherd" one layer of authority higher than themselves. This system is very similar to the so called "accountability groups" that the Promise Keepers use. Each Promise Keeper reports to a key man who then again reports to a level of authority that is higher than himself.

Some of the leaders of the Vineyard[73] church are also in key positions within the Promise Keepers organization. Rev. James Ryle, who is also McCartney's minister, is a member of the Promise Keepers board. Randy Phillips, president of the Promise Keepers, is also a member at Vineyard

---

[72] Amendment 2 was a state-wide anti-gay initiative prohibiting all branches of state government in Colorado from passing legislation or adopting policies prohibiting discrimination against lesbians and gay men based on their sexual orientation. The measure was passed by a slim majority of Colorado voters in 1992.

[73] Connected to the WOG is the WOG Vineyard Church, with a parish in Boulder, Colorado, where McCartney served as the head football coach. The Vineyard Church is known for its ultraconservative Protestantism which McCartney converted to from Catholicism. According to Bellant there is a big emphasis on signs, wonders and prophecy within the Vineyard Church. The leader of the church is John Wimber who describes his church as practicing "power evangelism" and his members as "self-conscious members of God's army that were sent to battle against the forces of the kingdom of darkness. One is either in God's Kingdom or Satan's."

Church. According to Bellant, "Never before have 300,000 men come together throughout human history except for the purpose of war." He claims to have experienced a vision where the Promise Keepers cleaned the United States of secularism.

The Promise Keepers are supposed to be organized by a system which brings men in local churches into groups of three to five. A "key man" heads every local group. These "key men" are chosen by the national organization and, ideally, have undergone training by it. John Swormly of the "Americans for Religious Liberty" organization and professor emeritus of social ethics at the St. Paul School of Theology writes that one of the seven promises of a Promise Keeper is to participate in small groups with other men and to monitor each other's behavior. This includes the most private aspects of everyone's life such as sexual relations, family life, business practices and financial affairs. The final goal is to have a key man in each one of the nation's 400,000 churches, as McCartney states, "whether they like it or not" (18). Cooperating pastors are being recruited and brought into the organizations. In 1996, the PK spent $4,600,00 in transportation, scholarships, lodging and meals to provide pastors of local churches with the things they needed in order to participate at the clergy conference in Atlanta. In comparison, an average ticket to a Promise Keeper event costs around $60 and does not include lodging or food.

The biggest event thus far that the Promise Keepers have held was the "Stand in the Gap Sacred Assembly of Men". An estimated 500,000 men came together to the Mall in Washington D.C. on October 4, 1997. Among other prominent Congressional Republicans who attended was the then Senate Majority Leader, Trent Lott.

A poll by the Washington Post found that 90% of the men present considered themselves fundamentalist, evangelical, or charismatic Christians. 46% of the participants said they were Republicans, 28% were Independents and 15% were Democrats. 61% declared themselves as conservative or very conservative, compared to about only one-third of the general population making this claim. Eight percent declared themselves as liberal or very liberal while 22% said they were moderate. Furthermore, 68% said that they had a positive opinion of the Christian Coalition, 60% had a negative opinion of feminists and 94% were opposed to letting same-sex couples get married.

At the end of the rally, McCartney gave a final speech that said "Obey your leaders and submit to their authority". Furthermore, he declared that the leaders he was referring to were the clergy and specifically only the male clergy.

The Promise Keepers' view on women and their role in marriage is the main concern to groups that have criticized the Promise Keepers. One of the most publicized statements from the PK comes from the manual "Seven Promises of a Promise Keeper". PK board of directors member Tony Evans, chaplain of the National Basketball Association team, the Dallas Mavericks, and according to the Toronto Star, a close confidante of George W. Bush, contributed the following:

> "...sit down with your wife and say something like this, 'Honey, I've made a terrible mistake...I gave up leading this family, and I forced you to take my place. Now I must reclaim that role.'...I'm not suggesting you ask for your role, I'm urging you to take it back...there can be no compromise here. If you're going to lead, you must lead...Treat the lady gently and lovingly. But lead!"

McCartney has issued statements with roughly the same content. He never speaks of married couples acting as peers in the relationship. It is always the man that is supposed to have the final say.

> "When there is a final decision that needs to be made and they can't arrive at one, the man needs to take responsibility," he says. "Every woman wants a guy like this -- a guy that has these things to offer and offers them tenderly and humbly, in the spirit of teamwork" (Stodghill et al. 1997).

The leaders of the Promise Keepers have made a point of saying that they strongly disagree with the notion that a woman should have the right to terminate a problem pregnancy. They also disagree that women should have the fundamental right as to when and if to become mothers. McCartney has been speaking for the aggressively anti-choice group "Operation Rescue".

Since 1998 attendance at Promise Keepers rallies has been dwindling to the point that their national organization had to lay off staff members. In 2002, the attendance at local events was down to 255,000 men, compared to 300,000 in 2000 and more than a million in 1996. Along with other organizations, Promise Keepers have been losing members, however, there is still a great potential of reaching men through their address data bases.

Second Chapter: Organizational Structures of the Religious Right

2.3. Leaders of the Religious Right

There is no doubt that many of the leaders of the Religious Right possess tremendous influence when it comes to motivating evangelicals to vote. In this section, I will provide a brief description of some of these leaders by highlighting shaping episodes of their lives. The approaches that the figures portrayed in this chapter use to influence people's political points of view range from open political rooting through political organizations, as in the case of Ralph Reed, to political influence through media where a political agenda is more subtle. Pat Robertson and James Dobson, although both major players in the political arena, are using very different strategies. Robertson uses overt persuasion through his Christian Broadcasting Network and the Christian Coalition while Dobson remains in the background appearing to be strictly a family therapist with no political agenda.

2.3.1. Marion "Pat" Robertson

Marion Gordon "Pat" Robertson was born and raised in Lexington, Virginia. His father was the well known Senator A. Willis Robertson, and his mother was a devout Christian. Robertson grew up a Baptist; however, he did not appear to be particularly religious in his youth. Utter (1995: 67) cite a "fondness for women, whiskey and poker." He graduated from Washington and Lee University as a Phi Beta Kappa student, studied at the University of London, served as a noncombatant with the Marines in Korea (1951-1952) and graduated from Yale Law School in 1955.

Robertson had a life-altering religious experience with the assistance of a fundamentalist friend of his mother's in 1956. Cornelius Vanderbreggen helped Robertson experience the Holy Spirit in what became the turning point of his career - a being "born-again" feeling. Robertson left his unsuccessful electronics business due to the feeling that his life was empty and meaningless and decided to become a minister.

He enrolled in the Biblical Seminary which later became the New York Theological Seminary in New York City. From 1956 to 1959 he transformed into a charismatic evangelical. While he was at the seminary, Robertson had contact with leaders of a Neo-Pentecostal renewal movement which taught him to experience "gifts of the Holy Spirit" such as

Glossolalia[74]. Some believe that the time Robertson spent at the seminary was the time in which his religious viewpoints and convictions were shaped. D.E. Harrel writes:

> "During the three-year period from 1956 to 1959 when Pat Robertson attended The Biblical Seminary and migrated from casual Christian, to fervent evangelical, to pioneering charismatic, his fundamental religious personality was formed."

According to Watson (1999: 31), although these "gifts of the Holy Spirit", which Robertson later used on his show, "The 700 Club" fit into the Pentecostal context, it does not mean that Robertson was ever a Pentecostal himself. He never actually became a member of any of the traditional Pentecostal denominations; he was ordained a Southern Baptist minister. However, it shows how the Charismatic movement was socially and ideologically different than the Pentecostal movement. Robertson's upbringing as the son of a well-off Democratic Senator and the innovative usage of a modern medium such as television, shows that the Charismatic movement was more willing to adapt to practical thought than the traditional Pentecostal movement.

When he left the Biblical Seminary, he returned to Virginia where he bought a television station in Portsmouth. This is where the Christian Broadcasting Network (CBN) began in 1960.

He set a goal in 1963 to enlist 700 listeners to pay $10 a month in order to cover the $7000 in expenses that the network had every month. This goal inspired Robertson to name his show "The 700 Club" and later "The 700 ClubProgram" which was based on the Johnny Carson Show. In 1965, Jim Bakker, whose capabilities in fund raising contributed immensely to the financial stability of the network, joined CBN and later went on to establish the PTL complex at Charlotte, North Carolina.

By 1975 CBN had grown immensely. There were an estimated 110 million viewers. Many of them were donating on a regular basis which enabled Robertson to build the International Headquarters Building and CBN University at Virginia Beach. They were opened in 1979. By 1987, the complex was employing over 4000 people on 380 acres of land. Robertson's charismatic style of healings and divine miracles in 1980 gave way to a more contemporary 700 Club. While religious experiences undoubtedly still

---

[74] Glossolalia: The art of speaking in tongues.

play the major role in this program, it has evolved to become more of a Christian news magazine.

As mentioned earlier, Robertson launched a campaign for the presidential elections in 1988 that Allan Hertzke (1993) calls "a populist crusade to return America to a sound moral footing". Robertson announced to viewers of the nationwide 700 Club that "If, by September 17, 1987, one year from today, three million registered voters have signed petitions telling me that they will pray, that they will work, that they will give toward my election, then I will run" (Boston 1996: 35-36). In addition to the positions mentioned in Chapter 3.3, he also opposed abortion with the reasoning that it reduced the number of births which consequently reduces the number of future taxpayers. These babies were needed to pay for the retirement of the baby boomers. He also supported the historical Religious Right theme of anti communism but ultimately focused on domestic issues.

According to James Penning, the Robertson supporters were "political amateurs – newly mobilized, ideologically-driven, and more committed to the candidate than to the party" while the supporters of the rival, George Bush, mainly consisted of "professionals" that were more pragmatic and more loyal to a party (Penning 1994).

Richard Cizik of the National Association of Evangelicals says:

> "Those who follow Robertson tend to feel discriminated against. They have a bunker mentality. They feel modernity is against them – in matters dealing with sex, crime, pornography, education." (Cizik in Penning 1994)

Considering that Robertson's religious background had high public visibility, it is not surprising that religious differences are quite notable between Robertson and Bush in the 1988 primaries. Looking at data from Michigan, South Carolina and Maine, Robertson relied heavily on charismatic Christians. Some other marked differences were the frequency of church attendance and the attitude towards foreign policy. While Bush and Robertson supporters were both showing pro-defense attitudes, Robertson supporters were more consistently doing so. However, Wilcox writes that "[t]hose who attended fundamentalist Baptist churches – the core base of the Moral Majority – were less supportive of Robertson than other whites" (Wilcox 2000).

Robertson's Personal Religious Convictions

Pat Robertson is a premillenialist[75] who expects that during his lifetime the end of the world will come; Jesus will return to earth and will set up his millennium reign. However, unlike other premillennialists, Robertson also believes in post tribulation rapture. In his understanding, Christians will have to live through the seven year tribulation on earth, before they will reign side by side with Jesus Christ during the millennium. Like many members of the Religious Right, he expresses the conviction that America holds a special relationship with God which is strengthened and maintained, only because there are so many Christians in the United States. Due to this special relationship, Robertson believes that God's judgment on the U.S. will be much milder than for other nations on this earth.

> "Yet God in my feeling is not going to judge America as harshly as He might because of the large numbers of Christians. Because of His elect in this nation He is going to spare the nation of the kind of judgment that some of the activities might deserve" (Robertson 1991).

As Robertson sees himself as "His elect", he perceives that it is his duty to work towards a socio-political order that is as close to being righteous and biblical as possible in order to make the judgment on the United States

---

[75] The Bible as the inerrant Scripture also hold for fundamentalists. From what many fundamentalists gather from reading the Bible, they expect the rapture to come at any time. They call themselves "pre-Tribulation dispensational premillennialists". Matthew 24:37-41 ("Then shall two be in the field; the one shall be taken, and the other left. Two women shall be grinding at the mill; the one shall be taken, and the other left.") in combination with 1 Thessalonians 4:15 – 18 ("caught up together with them in the clouds to meet the Lord in the air") in their opinion describes what is going to happen to the true believers: They will escape into heaven, while everybody else will have to suffer on earth. This "Rapture" is one of the most central themes in fundamentalist eschatology. Another important element is the belief that Christ will have to return to earth in order to establish a thousand-year reign on earth. Before this can happen, a period of trials and tribulation will take place on earth which will result in Armageddon, where the forces of good and evil wil meet.
Dispensationalism is a rather complicated issue as well. According to dispensationalists, the period between the birth of Jesus and the Rapture is called the "church age", one of seven periods that time in general is being divided into. During each period salvation is "dispensed" in distinct ways, however, during the "church age" salvation can be obtained by grace through belief in Jesus Christ. See also Ammerman 1998. For a fundamentalis point of view see the Scofield Reference Bible (1909). On "The Rapture" see: LaHaye, Tim and Jerry B. Jenkins. *Left Behind: A Novel of the Earths's Last Days*. Tyndale House Publisher. Wheaton, 1995.

milder. That the judgment is imminent seems to be clear to Robertson. However, his predictions that the tribulations would start in 1982 did not come true[76].

According to Watson (1999: 32), Robertson cannot be called a "fundamentalist" because his "word of knowledge" and extra biblical revelations would clash heavily with the inerrancy of the Bible. However, these extra biblical revelations have, as mentioned earlier, subsided in his broadcasting, while the resistance to the secularizing features of modernity has gotten stronger over the years. Whether Robertson has given up the charismatic approach in order to avoid intra-Christian particularism or whether it reflects him becoming more fundamentalist is difficult to judge. He describes himself as "an evangelical who believes in the gifts of the Holy Spirit" without describing what these gifts may mean to him.

Although Robertson's involvement in politics and government started early on due to his family background, he refused to support his father's unsuccessful reelection campaign in 1966. He named "divine guidance" as the prime factor for rejecting the involvement in politics after his religious conversion.

The candidacy of the born-again Christian Jimmy Carter made Robertson get involved in politics again. Social issues were becoming more important to him, and as he was getting more and more disappointed with President Carter, he "edged towards politics" as Watson (1999: 34) describes it. His friend, G. Conoly Philips, was a Democratic candidate running for Senate in Virginia. Robertson supported Philips who ultimately lost, but this support marks Robertson's first direct involvement in politics again, and his statements started to become more political. In an interview to U.S. News & World Report, he said that by taking both Catholics and Protestants into the equation "we have enough votes to run the country. And when the people say, 'We've had enough,' we are going to take over" (September 24, 1979: 37).

Robertson was heavily involved in the planning and also served as a co-chairman for the big rally in Washington D.C. on April 29, 1980 which was called the "Washington for Jesus" Rally. Although neither Billy Graham, nor Oral Roberts or Jerry Falwell participated, a large variety of evangelical leaders gave speeches at this event that drew between 200,000 and 500,000

---

[76] For a closer look at Pat Robertson's view on the Tribulation to come see: "The End of the Age", by Pat Robertson, published in 1995.

listeners (Harrel 1987: 177). They claimed it was a non political event; however, the organizers referred to the gathered crowd as "the great silent Majority". A few years later, Robertson said that the "Washington for Jesus" event was "the beginning of a spiritual revolution" which eventually "could sweep the nation" (Robertson 1986: 282). Ralph Reed stated that the event was very important in Robertson's decision to become more involved in politics: "While the purpose of the march was spiritual, the political subtext was unmistakable" (107). He further declares that Robertson's speech at the event was "a call for political action to turn the nation back from the brink of disaster."

Although Robertson apparently already saw possibilities for himself in the political field, he did not become involved in political causes at that point. He resigned from the board of directors of the Religious Roundtable, one of the earlier organizations of the Religious Right, in 1980 and according to Harrel (187), "severed all formal connection to the Christian Right organization."

This retreat from politics came at a time where Robertson expected the premillenial tribulation to come, and he might have wanted to concentrate his efforts on missionary work: "At least for the next couple of years the church of Jesus Christ should concentrate on the salvation of the lost, rather than taking over temporal political power" (in Mayer 1980: 36)[77].

The heavily influential Religious Right of the early 80's might have also played a role in the retreat for Robertson. Although he had his political ambitions, he might have seen that the Religious Right's quest for a theocratic America was not probable, because their political efforts seemed to be amateurish rather than professional. "The evangelists stand in danger of being used and manipulated," he said in Newsweek (Mayer 1980: 31). However, Robertson consistently gave speakers and leaders of the Religious Right opportunities to present their messages on The 700 Club.

---

[77] On various end-time prophecies see: Boyer, Paul. *When Time Shall Be No More: Prophecy Belief in Modern American Culture*. The Belknap Press of Harvard University Press. Cambridge, 1992. On date-setting: Oropeza, B.J. *99 Reasons Why No One Knows When Christ Will Return*. Inter Varsity Press. Downers Grove, 1994.

"Throughout the 1980's, CBN was perhaps the most valuable, consistent forum for New Right political figures eager to organize the fundamentalist masses. For years, everyone who was anyone in New Right political circles or in the U.S intelligence establishment (those not under deep cover) paraded through the 700 Club studios or spoke with Robertson live by satellite from one of CBN's off-site broadcast centers, usually in Washington, D.C." (Diamond 1989: 12).

By sympathizing with the Religious Right but distancing himself somewhat from it, Robertson was able to learn from their mistakes and wait for his time to come. The Freedom Council was meant to serve as a tool for future political ambitions. Robertson founded it in 1981, and it was meant to educate Christian activists on matters of political involvement. The Freedom Council only existed for five years but laid the groundwork for his presidential campaign.

The Robertson Candidacy

Robertson claims that he was resistant to the idea of running for president, even when he believed that he knew that this was God's plan for him. In his book "The Plan" which was published in 1989, he also states that he was urged to run for president by "numerous conservative, highly-placed friends" (20-23). He changed his party registration in 1984 to Republican, and in 1985 the Saturday Evening Post published an article in which a very positive picture of Robertson was painted. It emphasized his accomplishments in broadcasting from a business point of view, left out religious dogma and portrayed Robertson as the natural successor of Ronald Reagan.

It wasn't until October 1, 1987, however, that he officially announced his candidacy. He claimed that 3.3 million signatures had been gathered on behalf of him running for president. Although he lost in the end and was out of the race after March 8, 1988, this campaign can be seen as the transition from a more amateur to a more sophisticated way of lobbying in the political world.

Robertson's campaign was the first presidential campaign that was born out of religious enthusiasm. It was by no means smooth, and it had to cope with obstacles that were mainly self-inflicted. Statements that Robertson made during his campaign often seemed to be alleged misrepresentations and/or downright ridiculous. The scandals involving evangelical leaders that were taking place at that time did not help[78] and many of Robertson's views seemed, at the very least, unusual to the public. Although he managed to develop policies on a broad spectrum of issues, his main topic was morality, and his issues were wrapped around that. When, however, the truth about his alleged military accomplishments surfaced[79], his own morality was highly questioned which made it even more difficult for him to appeal to any voters beyond the evangelical spectrum.

His basic campaign speech was free of biblical citations (Watson 1999: 36). Nevertheless, his campaign evoked strong feelings, both in the pro- and in the anti-Robertson communities. For the pro-Robertsons, his candidacy was a candidacy for God as well as for their country, and many supporters linked biblical prophecies to it. While maybe amateurish, many of those supporters could not have been more enthusiastic about the campaign which, in their minds, almost equaled a crusade, and they, therefore, showed strong emotional involvement.

But exactly these overt expressions of faith and beliefs made Robertson suspicious for the other side of the spectrum that feared that a successful campaign would pose a threat to freedom and was paving the way towards theocracy. Equally emotional, they formed a strong anti-Robertson group. The speech that Robertson gave to formally announce his candidacy was accompanied by protesters who were attempting to shout Robertson down and were carrying signs that read "Hitler in '39, Robertson in '88" (Schribman 1989: A44).

The morality that Robertson was referring to was closely linked to the idea of a "Christian America" which in Robertson's, and many of the supporters of the Religious Right's[80], opinion was lost during the 60's. This loss that he describes as the "tailspin in morality" also represents the coming of the "antichrist spirit".

---

[78] See Chapter 1.3
[79] Robertson had to drop a suit in which he claimed that an account of how his father kept him out of combat in the Korean war was false (Wilcox 2000)
[80] See Chapter 1.2

"The people in a society begin to throw off the restraints of history, then the restraints of written law, then accepted standards of morality, then established religion, and, finally, God Himself" (Robertson, 1982: 29).

For Robertson, morality is equivalent to self-restraint. As soon as self-restraint is abandoned, self-indulgence and, therefore, immorality takes over. But Robertson does not talk about general morality or general values. In his mind, morality is equivalent to religion, and not just any religion but the Christian religion. Thus, the reinstatement of morality really means the reinstatement of "Christian America". In his book "America's Date with Destiny", Robertson draws a picture of early American history as being especially blessed by God due to the strong Christian faith of its founders. However, during much of the 20th century Robertson observed the withdrawal of God's special blessing, because the strong faith of the founders was replaced by a much weaker faith of the following generations. He claims that "national impotence", immorality, irreligion and anarchy have taken over and have brought America to a tragic decline (Robertson 1986: 296f).

In Robertson's point of view, the only way to save America is to hope to be blessed by God again. To accomplish that the entire nation would have to repent and return to righteousness. The way to repent would be an evangelical involvement in politics (Robertson, ibid).

Although Robertson, on occasion, has made statements that would suggest he accepts and believes in a separation of church and state , many other statements have hinted that he would like a stronger influence of religion on government. In a November 1985 interview with US News & World Report he says that the church and state, as institutions, shouldn't influence each other. He continued to say that he thinks that there should be moral influences and that deeply religious people should be involved in the governmental process. "I certainly don't think the Constitution in any way intended to protect the government from religion" (U.S. News & World Report, November 4, 1985: 75).

On January 11, 1985 on his show The 700 Club he said,

"Individual Christians are the only ones really – and Jewish people, those who trust the God of Abraham, Isaac and Jacob – are the only ones that are qualified to have the reign, because hopefully they will be governed by God and submitted to him" (*The 700 Club*. Christian Broadcasting Network, January 11, 1985).

When asked about this statement later on, he confirmed that he meant that the only ones eligible for office and government were Christians and Jews (King 1987: 1). At best, Robertson's position can be described as ambiguous. Apparently he changed his message substantially, depending on who he delivered a speech to (Hume 1986: 44).

Generally speaking, Robertson depicted himself as being the victim of religious bigotry. He accused People for the American Way of attacking him so that they could "destroy all the faith and all the beliefs of the evangelical people in this country". He claimed that the anti-Catholicism of the 1960's was somewhat the same as what was happening to him during his campaign: "What they said in 1960 about Kennedy was bigotry. What's being said about me in 1988 is bigotry" (New York Times, February 10, 1988: l22).

Robertson founded the Christian Coalition in 1989, and from then on, his political activities were closely linked to this organization which is explored in Chapter 2.2.1. However, from the very beginning of the 2000 presidential campaign, Robertson supported George W. Bush. Not only did he endorse Bush on The 700 Club, he also tape recorded a phone message in the GOP primaries in which he attacked the campaign manager for McCain, former GOP senator Warren Rudman[81]. The taped phone messages were delivered to social conservative voters in Michigan and, ultimately, made national

---

[81] Robertson called former GOP senator Warren Rudman, who was McCain's campaign manager in New Hampshire, a "vicious bigot". He accused him of making derogatory comments about the Religious Right. Rudman's point of view on potential presidential candidate, Colin Powell, was not popular with the Religious Right who would not have supported such a candidacy due to Powell's pro-life record and possibly due to his African American ethnicity. Rudman publicly criticized the Religious Right for its opposition to such a candidacy. Robertson had to back off of his accusation later on and stated "I may have gone on that phrase a little too far" ("Who's a Bigot?" Washington Post, February 24, 2000, p. A20).

headlines and were cited as an example for the tactics of the Religious Right. The Bush campaign was not pleased and called on Robertson to make his rhetoric more moderate.

Robertson supported Bush for more than one reason. As George Bush was the candidate that came from the establishment of the GOP, he also seemed to be the most likely to unite different wings. His emphasis on depicting himself as a born-again Christian who had gone through troubled times in his younger years but had been redeemed by Jesus read like one of the success stories that Robertson would frequently have people talk about on The 700 Club. Moreover, by supporting Bush early on, Robertson, who has proven his tactical approach at politics as I have described above, might have seen a chance for personal power when backing the most likely candidate. In addition, Senator McCain put a strong emphasis on campaign finance reform, which, if successful, would have posed a major financial threat to the Christian Coalition. Although McCain's and Bush's pro-life stance on abortion was clearly documented by past voting behavior, Robertson falsely suggested that McCain was actually not a supporter of pro-life. As Rozell writes (2000: 7), Robertson's attacks were at times on a very personal level, claiming that McCain did not have the moral and emotional stability that it takes to be president.

In April 2001, Robertson made remarks regarding China's policy on forced abortions which caused an uproar within the Religious Right. He stated that, although not supporting it, he could understand China's policy on abortion and that it was vital for the survival of the culture. He, furthermore, elaborated on the racial purity of the Han Chinese instead of onthe unborn babies, which had usually been his emphasis in earlier comments on abortion (Wilcox 2002: 119). He suggested that with many female fetuses being aborted, there might be a need to "import" Indonesian women in order to carry on that particular people.

Robertson left the Christian Coalition later that year with much of his former influence gone. However, he is still present via the 700 Club. Besides the fact that he is now selling "Pat's Age Defying Protein Shake", his comments on American Politics keep astonishing the public. In October 2003 he stunned listeners with the statement that the United States Department of State should be destroyed by a nuclear bomb in order "to take care of the problems that the people inside cause us".

2.3.2. Ralph Reed

Although Ralph Reed left the Christian Coalition in April of 1997, he has undoubtedly shaped it most profoundly. Reed was born as Ralph Eugene Reed, Jr., on June 24, 1961 in Portsmouth, Virginia. Throughout his youth, the Reed family moved frequently with stops in Miami, Florida; Louisville, Kentucky; and Toccoa, Georgia due to his father's employment with the U.S. Navy. Showing an early interest in politics and history, as a teenager he ran a direct-mail campaign for a student council (Plotz http://slate.msn.com/id/1819).

He attended the University of Georgia from 1979 to 1983 and became involved with the College Republicans, the debating society and the college newspaper (Barret 1993: 58). In 1980, he was a volunteer for the campaigning of Ronald Reagan and the Republican candidate for a U.S. Senate seat from Georgia, Mack Mattingly. It was Mattingly that he interned with in the summer in Washington D.C. before spending the fall semester there with the College Republicans and the Republican National Committee.

When returning to College, more ambitious than ever, he was accused of plagiarizing a story that he had written for the college newspaper which cost him his job there (Conason 1992: 139). However, upon graduating from college in 1983, he won the prize for best senior essay in History at the University of Georgia.

After graduation, he returned to Washington D.C. where he became the College Republican's executive director. In his book "Politically Incorrect", he describes how he became disillusioned after seeing how practical politics work and specifically after seeing how one pro-life, pro-family politician was having an extramarital affair. He writes "The lofty ideals that I brought to the nation's capital were shaken by the reality of life in Congress. I learned quickly that the pursuit of power is an empty and unsatisfying exercise without a moral compass to guide one's journey" (25).

In September of 1983, he had a religious experience while attending a worship service which turned him into an evangelical Christian and which, according to him, changed his life dramatically (1994: 26). As many before him - including Robertson - he gave up drinking, smoking and the use of profanity. Opposite to Robertson, Reed has always kept his religious profile low, sometimes referring to his faith as charismatic, sometimes belonging to the Pentecostals and sometimes belonging to the Presbyterians (Sedgwick 1995: 40). Since his ambitions have always seemed to have been more political than religious, it seems probable, that he has been trying to evade excluding denominations by defining his faith too narrowly. By doing so, he has attracted social conservatives from the catholic faith more so than Robertson has done in the past.

Reed stayed with the College Republicans until North Carolina Senator, Jesse Helms, ran again for Senate. This reelection campaign prompted Reed to move to North Carolina where he helped Helms by initiating a conservative students' organization the "Students for America" (SFA). Time Magazine describes it as "a conservative organization with an evangelical tint" (Barret 1993: 58) while an undated pamphlet published by SFA says that "[they] are patriotic conservative students dedicated to the advancement of Judeo-Christian values. [... We are] the vanguard of the conservative movement on the college campuses and the fastest growing youth political movement in the nation"[82].

After the successful campaign for Jesse Helms, Reed decided to leave politics, because he thought it was too unstable for a career. Instead he enrolled in Emory University's Ph.D. program for history. He graduated in 1991, however, in 1989 he met Pat Robertson for the first time at a banquet in Washington D.C. Robertson told him of his plan to launch a new Religious Right organization, since Jerry Falwell's Moral Majority was not doing particularly well and since he thought its end was soon to come[83]. Reed, according to Time Magazine, wrote a memorandum on what such an organization could look like and became its executive director that same year. Although Reed had supported Jack Kemp rather than Pat Robertson in the 1988 primaries, Robertson knew of Reed's evangelical conversion because The 700 Club had broadcasted a short film on it as part of its "conversion stories" series (Barret 1993: 59).

In accordance with Robertson's tactic, the messages Reed tells people inside and outside his organization are very different: To the mainstream he claims that all the Christian Coalition wants is to be part of the discussion. However, he told fans of the Christian Coalition in Charleston, South Carolina: "Our ambition is to be larger and more effective than both political parties combined" (Barret 1993: 59).

---

[82] While there are still some local chapters operating today, there appears to be little evidence of a nationally run Students for America. No webpage or listings as an active organization could be found by the author.

[83] See Chapter 2.2.1.

In 1997 Reed announced his withdrawal from the Christian Coalition. He remained on the board, but opened his own political consulting firm, Century Strategies. Its agenda is to support candidates that agree with the Christian Coalition's stands on all issues as well as to broaden its base with the general public. "We have enjoyed enormous success in the arena of issue politics," he told Time Magazine. "In order to take that forward to its logical conclusion, we have to have the same measure of success in winning elections" (Barret 1993: 60).

In the 2000 election campaign, Reed joined Robertson early on by supporting George W. Bush in his candidacy. According to Rozell (2000: 3) this support meant little to the grass-roots activists of the Christian Coalition since Reed and Robertson were seen as pragmatists rather than as the movement's true core. The lure of power and influence by supporting the most likely candidate to succeed who was also pro-life, pro-family and was credible due to his voting record from early on, might have contributed to Reed and Robertson's sign of support rather than the actual belief that George Bush was the ideal candidate.

Furthermore, Reed had been hired by the Bush administration to do mass mailings on Bush's behalf; however, as the Washington Post revealed, Reed also seemed to have served as a connection between Bush and Microsoft. Reed had been hired in 1998 to rally grass-roots support for the software giant as it was facing a long court battle with charges filed by 19 states and the Justice department (Grimaldi 2000: A4).

Reed has withdrawn from the spotlight; however, his old connections and experience in the political arena will make him an important factor behind the scenes.

2.3.3. James C. Dobson

James Dobson is the head of the Religious Right organization "Focus on the Family". Son of a Nazarene minister who was finishing off his schooling during Dobson's childhood, James Dobson lived with his aunt and uncle, who was a minister himself, for much of his upbringing.

Nazarene ministry requires a calling from God himself, and due to the fact that Dobson never experienced that calling, he decided to take a more worldly approach. He attended Pasadena College in California which is a Nazarene school. Afterwards, he enrolled in the graduate program for

Psychology at the University of Southern California. It was child psychology he went into. He worked in this field for 14 years as a professor for pediatrics at the University of Southern California of Medicine and for 17 years on the attending staff at the Children's Hospital in L.A.

Dobson hosts a daily radio program where he gives advice to families. For this, he uses his own mixture of theology, psychology, humanism and common sense. However, he rarely relies on biblical verses, but still supports and emphasizes traditional Christian values. 28 million people hear his radio broadcasts each week with 4 million listening to the Focus on the Family broadcast each day. His books have sold more than 16 million copies. His vast amounts of tracts and pamphlets are too numerous to count.

Although few people outside the circle of the Religious Right actually know his name, Dobson, without a doubt, is one of the most influential personas of it, or as Meryem Ersoz, in her essay "Gimme That Old-Time Religion", claims "[...]one of the most powerful men in America" (Ersoz 1998: 222).

ABC's Day One news show did a fifteen minute special on Dobson and his organization. In order for Dobson to cooperate, he demanded to put his own camera behind the ABC camera, so he could use this filming for his own purposes later on. Dobson took 3 of his 30-minute daily broadcastings to dissect the ABC segment and to give it his own spin. Dobson claims that "we weren't quite sure what the media would do," and by doing so, presented himself as a possible victim going up against a Goliath. However, Dobson's empire hardly makes him a David. In the end, Dobson admitted that the interview conducted by ABC was "an honest effort to describe the ministry of Focus on the Family"[84]. However, Dobson then produced his own videotape that could be ordered for "a gift of $7" from the Focus of the Family group. It contains commentaries on the broadcast and inserts parts of the interview that had not been shown in the fifteen minute segment by ABC.

The influence of his radio broadcast becomes especially significant when it is used to mobilize political activists and, therefore, translates directly into political action (Ersoz 1998: 218). According to the Day One broadcast on Focus on the Family from September 30th, 1995, Dobson can mobilize more political action than Pat Robertson can through his 700 Club.

---

[84] James Dobson during the September 30, 1995 edition of the Focus on the Family broadcast.

This explains the power that Dobson, who says of himself that he is not involved in any political activities and merely wants to "inform" rather than influence voters, holds in Washington. However, in a March 1995 letter to his supporters Dobson warns against the Republican Party becoming "increasingly squishi on the issue of abortion", mentioning Senator Bob Dole in particular. He then goes on threatening to not vote for any Republican candidate who is not firmly against abortion.

> "I am commited never again to cast a vote for a politician who would kill one innocent baby. These little ones have no defense except that which we provide for them. Never will I use my influence, however remotely, to support the shedding of their blood...By voting for a moderate pro-abortionist who might be more desirable in the short run, we squander our influence on decision makers. Rather, when a significant number of votes are cast for a third party/pro-life candidate, even in a losing cause, that fact will not go unnoticed by political leaders. They will be more likely to court our support in the future, especially if they lost the last election. That's the way the game is played." (Dobson 1995).

In February 1998, Dobson flexed his muscle again, threatening to leave the Republican party, saying he would take the majority of some 28 million listeners with him (Carney 1998). The GOP responded promptly. In the House, the legislative agenda was crammed with "pro-family" votes aimed at Dobson's constituency.

3. The Campaign

3.1. Channels and Mechanisms of Influence

Apart from the influence that the media has on voting behavior, how does the Religious Right reach its constituents? A central role is being played by local churches and their ministers. I will show the link between churches and political institutions.

3.1.1. Connecting Congregations to Political Processes

How is it possible for evangelical churches to influence their members? There are two main ways to connect the constituents to the political process. First of all, institutional participation, which the church as an institution would qualify for, builds, as Greenberg (2000: 377) calls it, "social capital"[113]. Through similar norms, trust and building networks, participants are enabled to pursue common objectives. A shared faith acts as the lowest common denominator in the religious category, with moral norms in the social category being the next step. It can certainly work the other way around as well. Social norms can lead an individual to a certain congregation and finally to a certain faith[114]. The shared norms mentioned above underlie a strong polity and civic engagement.

Second of all, local groups[115], such as congregations, often represent part of a broader institutional network. These institutions provide political information and/or participatory resources which, in the end, mobilize people to take action.

---

[113] Greenberg refers to the term "social capital" going back to Robert Putnam. For Greenberg the term reflects "the features of social life—networks, norms and trust—that enable participants to act together more effectively to pursue shared objectives". (Greenberg 2000). See also Putnam, Robert. "Tuning In, Tuning Out.: The Strange Disappearance of Social Capital in America". In: PS: *Political Science and Politics* 28 (December 1995), and Ammerman, Nancy T. Congregation and Community. Rutgers University Press. New Brunswick, 1997.

[114] Certainly there are many more factors that come into question when developing one's faith. Family background, location, demographic factors, etc.; however, in this context, this paper will be limited to aspects of the social and political sphere.

[115] Even the free evangelical churches, which concentrate on being independent of a larger organization such as the ELCA and which put a personal relationship with God before any other relationship within or outside the church, have an organization that connects all of them. In the United States, this organization is the EFCA, the Evangelical Free Church of America.

Third Chapter: The Campaign

Since the very beginning of the United States, churches and denominations have been an important influence on the political landscape. The abolition movement was closely linked to the Quakers, evangelical churches were heavily involved in the temperance movement, the antiwar movement of the 1960's drew many of its supporters from mainline protestant churches and many important resources were generated by the black churches for the Civil Rights movement. The Shaker movement in the New England States found its form of community living to be a utopian life style[116]. More recently, the Religious Right and its grassroots efforts around certain topics such as abortion and school curricula have been successful at connecting religion and politics.

All of these examples draw attention to the fact that religious institutions are indeed independent political actors that influence public policy as well as personal political preferences and behavior[117]. In society, churches are the link between public and private life. They simultaneously purvey private values and norms but also serve as arbiters of social relations. As a connector between the state and the individual, they provide a space where discussion on either the state or values and norms can take place. Dominant cultural discourse can be viewed and counter measures can be discussed before entering the area of collective action.

Robert Putnam (1995: 66) states that the performance of representative governments is being improved by networks of civic engagement since they foster an interest in the collective good. Religious institutions are part of such a network of associations which bolster democratic governance. However, they also create challenges to dominant groups and discourses. Authority can be challenged, as in the Civil Rights movement, and can be translated into legislation that is helping the cause. When it comes to the

---

[116]The Shakers, named after their habit of dancing throughout their services, still have a few societies left in the United States. Their community life consists of the strict division between women and men, who only see each other during church and some communal work. New members are only acquired by outsiders, possibly with children of their own, to join the denomination. The Shakers are, technologically, a very advanced society as opposed to the Amish, for example. They have been credited with the development of washing machines, for example. Until this day, furniture with a functional design often has Shaker elements to it. See also Brewer, Priscilla J. *Shaker Communities, Shaker Lives.* University Press of New England. Boston, 1988. and Merton, Thomas and Paul M. Pearson (Eds.). <u>Seeking Paradise: The Spirit of the Shakers</u>. Orbis Books. Chicago, 2003.

[117] See also: Hertzke, Allen D. *Representing God in Washington: The Role of Religious Lobbies in the American Polity.* Knoxville: University of Tennessee Press, 1988.

Third Chapter: The Campaign

Religious Right, Greenberg (2000: 380) argues that "the challenge is to discern the ways that religious institutions translate this social capital into concrete political and social action."

As mentioned above, the church can influence the opinions of the leaders and serve as a source of political information. Since religious involvement is linked to political attitudes, churches can influence political behavior on an individual level. In order to understand political decision making, the individual's social context has to be taken into consideration. This involves, but is not limited to, as Greenberg (2000: 380) notes, the daily life as well as the influence of discussion networks. In this context, bible study groups, mother and child groups, and so called "prayer breakfasts" that are held on a weekly basis in some congregations come to mind. In addition, some non-faith related activities that are being performed within the same community may play a role as well, for example trips to sporting events or the upkeep of the church property and equipment. All these occasions present opportunities for discussing political and/or faith related topics with peers which has a reinforcing effect.

Milbrath and Goel (1977) argue that there is a strong link between church attendance and voter turnout, politics in church and political knowledge. Churches are a location where social interaction occurs frequently and regularly with a somewhat limited pool of participants. Leaders and congregational members exert and succumb to considerable amounts of pressure as far as behavioral norms and social matters are concerned. Particularly in evangelical churches which are often more closely knit than mainstream protestant churches, it is of great interest what types of lifestyle other family members of the congregation are leading, and conformity can be a crucial factor for acceptance[118].

---

[118] See also: Oscar B. Martison and E.A. Wilkening, "Religious Participation and Involvement in Local Politics throughout the Life Cycle," Sociological Forces 20 (October 1987) 309-18

According to Greenberg[119], who conducted a study in this field, clerical and lay leaders alike were constantly sending out the message "love thy neighbor", "don't be a bench member", or "reach out to people in need". This occurred in sermons and in informal meetings or activities. Furthermore, in bible study classes where implications for daily life are being studied, these types of messages are being supported by immediate biblical evidence which is much closer to the individual who can then look up and read for themselves the individual text passages. Rather than being preached to from the pulpit, members can discuss with each other in bible classes, usually under the guidance of a clerical leader, who can point out bible passages that seem important to the matter and to the leader.

3.1.2. Faith and Politics

When clerical leaders make a connection between living a Christian life and achieving political goals, congregational members are being encouraged to act on their faith in the political arena[120]. Part of the criteria for living "a Christian life" is acting in the political sphere, as many religious leaders[121] are emphasizing. In their world view, public life is corrupt, and by entering the political sphere, Christians can work towards a less secular and,

---

[119] Greenberg's study was aimed at exploring possibilities and limitations when it comes to religious institutions and political influence. She collected data in extensive field research in Protestant churches in Chicago, Illinois by conducting in depth interviews and observation of various worship services and activities at eight churches across racial and teological traditions. She visited one black mainline church, two white mainline churches, three black evangelical churches and two white evangelical churches. Greenbergs respondents were all Protestant women. For more information on her study see Greenberg, Anna. "The Church and the Revitalization of Politics and Community." *Political Science Quarterly*, Vol. 115, 2000

[120] This approach signals a turnaround in evangelical doctrine since the traditional approach to politics was very reserved. This reservation was rooted a) in the conviction that politics were a worldly matter in which true Christians would only be subjected to sin by the appeal of political power and influence and b) in the teachings of premillennialism which is the belief that in order for Christ to return, the world has to be "on its knees" with conditions for the people that are basically hell on earth.

[121] James Dobson is a religious leader in this context as well. Dobson, who has no theological education and emphasizes in his daily radio show that his theological knowledge is limited, relies to some degree on the bible to explain his views on child rearing. He uses the fact that he is not theologically educated to bolster his "common knowledge" image that he presents to the outside world.

thus, more honorable and "Godly" political work. Christian voices need to be heard in order for politics to go in the direction which will advance the Christian causes. Clerical leaders support this approach by giving out information on political issues and participatory opportunities. They are linking norms of civic engagement with the chance to act politically.

This channel of religious influence on the political sphere can be very efficacious, as it provides incentives to act politically on several levels. First of all, the religious conscious of the individual is being stimulated by the pure mentioning of political issues which are being debated within the religious community or congregation. Secondly, group pressure will likely push an individual towards action in the political field, especially if clerical and secular leaders of a congregation pull in the same direction. Verba, Schlozman and Brady (1995) found in their study on civic voluntarism in American Politics that people are more likely to hear political appeals and encouragement at church than in other settings[122]. Thirdly, the political information members of the congregation are receiving is filtered by clerical or secular leaders. Therefore, members can be influenced just by the choice of topics that are being discussed.

Each of these mechanisms reinforces the other mechanisms, which means that this channel can be very influential. Greenberg (2000: 381) argues that "[t]hese instances of political communication, therefore, underlie political action as they provide both incentives to become active in public life and information to enable efficacious participation in politics".

3.1.3. Clerical Encouragement

Considering that the church is ostensible as a nonpolitical institution, political issues are being handled in church quite frequently. Verba, Schlozman and Brady (1995: 19) argue that twenty-five percent of their sample, reports hearing statements on political issues from the pulpit[123]. Greenberg (2000: 382) concludes that this type of political information and exhortation leads to greater involvement in political matters for members of the congregation.

---

[122] 34% of the people polled stated that they've been asked to vote or to participate in political matters at churches compared to 19% on the job and 9% in other nonpolitical organizations.

[123] Verba, Schlozman and Brady conducted a survey on citizen participation in 1995. See: Verba, Sidney, Kay Lehman Schlozman, and Henry E. Brady. *Voice and Equality: Civic Voluntarism in American Politics*. Harvard University Press. Cambridge, 1995

Third Chapter: The Campaign

The two dimensions of political involvement in church are the promotion and facilitation of civic engagement. The community outreach will be emphasized by the clerical and secular leaders of a church, because they believe that it is important that Christian voices are heard in public life. Participation in politics, such as voting or contacting government officials, is the main goal in this area. However, there are churches which are more active. In these congregations, the encouragement requires a more demanding involvement: Sponsorship of political action or building coalitions with other local, political organizations. Local party committees or school boards are an example of such attempts. Trans-denominational organizations such as Christian Women[124], the Christian Coalition or Concerned Women for America also recruit volunteers via these channels.

3.1.4. Community Outreach

Community outreach is another area where church involvement encourages political action. Many clerical leaders state that it is an important part of Christian life to help the less fortunate. Active participation in communal efforts or social welfare ministries becomes political, because members of the congregation interact with government officials through agencies of the state. When ministries expose people to social and economic problems, participants are more likely to get involved in political action, because it will make them more aware of the policy-making process (Ammerman 1997).

Ministerial involvement is usually triggered by the perspective that the world is in a horrible state which needs immediate improvement (Greenberg 2000). Especially the state of political life, which many ministers in Greenberg's study are disgusted by, needs immediate change. Another area

---

[124] Christian Women is especially active in the rural Midwest. The meetings that I have attended were centered on prayer, some hymnal singing and usually some sort of lunch. They took place in a community center in rural southern Minnesota, instead of in a church basement which is common in Trans denominational and evangelical congregations. After the food was served, a speaker gave a lecture on a certain topic. Although the topics usually evolved around trials and tribulations that individuals had gone through with the help of God, each speech had a part where political aspects of American life were mentioned. Whether it was the typical topics such as abortion or "special rights" for homosexuals or something centered on patriotism and how to express the love to one's country, the attending women seemed to think nothing of the political content of those speeches coming from a Christian organization. The meetings I attended were pre 9/11 and still took place during the late Clinton years.

of improvement is the embattled status of Christians in the public sphere. These ministers emphasize the part that every Christian, in their opinion, has to play in the political sphere in order to live a "true Christian life". One white[125] evangelical pastor says:

> "[T]hat's where we are as a church. I see our responsibility to be information givers. But mainly [we] have to be a motivator to get individuals to play their role in society nationally." (Greenberg 2000: 383).

All ministers in Greenberg's study believe that sermons with political content and informational materials are necessary to live a true Christian life. In addition, they all give political organizations access to their congregation. For mainstream clerical leaders, this was as far as they would go; they would not allow partisan or ideological politics to take place in the religious setting.

White evangelical leaders, however, used tactics to circumvent opposition to excessively partisan politics. They allowed conservative political groups to distribute score cards on the candidates. The conservative score cards generally selected issues where only the conservative candidates would be able to produce positive scores. Although no candidate was explicitly mentioned as the one to vote for, given the outcome of the score cards, only the conservative one could expect a vote. Some churches allow "teach-ins" by anti-abortion activists who, in addition, can leave brochures and leaflets in the back of the chapel. One organization, the Illinois Citizens for Life, leaves brochures at churches. These brochures list ways and opportunities for members of the congregation to become active in the political sphere through letter writing, candidate information gathering, as well as citizen lobbying trips to Springfield and Washington.

Churches have the resources and the power to get their congregation involved in political action. Viewed in an isolated way, however, individual churches rarely sponsor political action against the government or the state. What does take place is that the infrastructure is being used for other, more political organizations. The networks that religious institutions are embedded in also act as providers of political action (Ammerman 1997).

---

[125] Greenberg found differences between mainly Caucasian and mainly African American ministers in opinions on political participation. For more information see Greenberg 2000.

Third Chapter: The Campaign

Community outreach projects involve people in the church that are not typically members of the congregation. When churches are providing space for community activity they again reach out to people who would otherwise never enter a particular church. These networks that are being built have extensive consequences. When members of a church are also members of a political organization, they can rely on these structures and "word gets out" without much additional organizational effort. Churches, thus, empower community groups which then interact with state organizations in order to influence policy making for social problems.

Although the approximately 300,000 (Greenberg 2000) congregations in the continental United States provide education and worshipping services as their main task for their members, a great majority is also involved in one or more kinds of community outreach programs. These programs are things such as having the different congregations of a community deliver "meals on wheels" or installing the "buddy program" which brings children of working parents together with adult "buddies" that spend a certain amount of time with them in order to help them adapt better to society.

The Independent Sector's national survey of religious institutions[126] found that congregations have a wide area of services they provide:

- Human Services, 87% (meal services)
- International outreach, 79% (refugee programs)
- Public or societal benefit, 70% (community development)
- Health, 68% (institutional care)
- Arts, 43%
- Culture and education, 38%
- Environmental improvement, 27%

These services are generally being provided outside the churches. Visitations to sick members of the community or driving people to their

---

[126] The Independent Sector, in conjunction with the Gallup Organization, conducted a survey on approximately 4,205 congregations in 1987. For further reading see: From Belief to Commitment: The Activities and Finances Of Religious Congregations in the United States (Washington, DC: The Independent Sector, 1988)

destinations are not included in this survey and would add a certain percentage.

In a survey that the organization Partner for Sacred Places[127] conducted, it was found that 91 percent of all congregations have some type of community services. Each congregation, on average, hosted 4 different types of programs. In addition, 81 percent of the beneficiaries of these programs were not involved in the congregations that conducted them. 45 percent of the congregations opened their spaces up to other groups with additional contributions such as funding and in-kind support.

Due to the fact that the Republican Congress mandated charitable choice in the welfare reform law of 1996 and because Bush is pushing the Charitable Choice act to be applicable to all federally-funded human services program, these numbers are likely to increase even further in the years to come.

The Independent Sector survey found numbers that show even stronger support for the larger community. Here, 60 percent of the churches surveyed made space available to non-church groups one day or more per week.

Sharing space with other groups and organizations offers great potential for involvement in political action. Just by selecting the groups, e.g. pro-choice vs. pro-life, a congregation influences communal politics. By linking governmental programs with church based outreach projects, as the Charitable Choice act promotes, these provisions are likely to change the relationship of churches to public policy making, because churches will then be in closer consultation with the state. Also, these provisions create incentives for congregations to compete for this government money. George W. Bush is talking about fierce competition between churches for this state money: "I envision a new welfare system, an energized, competitive program where a person who needs help would get a debit card, redeemable not just at a government agency, but at the Salvation Army or a church day-care facility" (Christian Science Monitor, April 22, 1997).

---

[127] Partners for Sacred Places is involved in the conservation and preservation of historically significant holy sites and religious properties. For the survey, in which 113 randomly selected congregations took part, see: Diane Cohen and A. Robert Jaeger, Sacred Places at Risk: New Evidence on How Endangered Older Churches and Synagogues Serve Communities. Philadelphia: Partners for Sacred Places, 1997.

3.1.5. White Evangelical Churches

White evangelical churches are least likely to address urgent social and economic problems in their own community. Usually their efforts are concentrated on evangelism and "spreading the word" rather than dealing with other communities. The political agenda of the evangelical churches is commonly centered on a particular political agenda which mainly deals with family issues. Grassroots mobilization is one of their greatest strengths, because they often concentrate on one issue, for example, abortion and will get much involvement from other members of the congregation. According to the Independent Sector, evangelical congregations are usually involved in programs or services that are limited to counseling, recreational activities for children, refugee-related programs, and right-to-life activities. Wuthnow (1997: 14) argues that there is no relationship between the involvement with civic organizations or volunteer work outside of the church setting and church attendance. Within evangelical Protestantism, social outreach is often seen as a necessary means to free families from some of their problems in order to make them more susceptible to being evangelized. If a family is worried about making ends meet or other such matters, faith and life in Christ will be of less importance than earning money.

These forms of protestant churches have been constantly growing since the 1970's at a rate that is faster than the growth rate of liberal or moderate churches. In Minnesota for example[128], data from the fall of 2002 showed that there were more evangelical congregations than mainline protestant ones (Star Tribune, Evangelical Christianity Comes of Age, March 3, 2003, pp 01A)[129].

---

[128] The free (Hosanna Free Lutheran Church) evangelical church that I have attended in rural Minnesota was founded in the mid 90's. Apparently the town with a population of 4,300 people, had a need for an even more conservative church. Currently, there are 19 churches in the small town, and the free evangelical church has approximately 80 members. Its congregation is mainly made up of people who felt that the ELCA was too liberal, which some members summarize with the words "The ELCA is pro-homosexuality and pro-abortion." That is certainly not the case; however, the ELCA tries to be an inclusive organization that welcomes all believers. They are in the process of coming to a conclusion of what their standpoints on these issues are. See www.elca.org.

[129] Minnesota's new Republican governor Tim Pawlenty belongs to an evangelical denomination in the Twin Cities. The national meeting of the National Association of Evangelicals (NAE) was held in March of 2003 at his exact church. The main speaker was James Towey, Director of the White House Office of Faith Based Initiatives.

Third Chapter: The Campaign

3.2. Aspects of the Financing of the 2000 Campaign

As the 2000 elections were drawing closer, it became more and more evident that this particular election would be a very close one. In an effort to ensure that the campaign committees of each party had enough money to spend on the candidates, fund raising became essential at every level of the election. In the end, the fund raising and the money spent in the 2000 presidential election exceeded every previous election ever held in the United States.

Al Gore, as the incumbent Vice-President of the United States, was mostly unchallenged in his quest for the Democratic Party candidacy. His two competitors never posed a threat to his campaign within the Democratic Party. George Bush, on the other hand, had to beat 10 other candidates even though he was a very visible candidate.

3.2.1. The Bush Approach

George W. Bush was the first major-party presidential candidate who did not accept public funding and was, therefore, exempt from the terms and regulations that came with such an acceptance. Consequently, he raised more than $100 million in private contributions. In comparison, only four years earlier, Bob Dole, the Republican presidential candidate in 1996, "only" raised $50.7 million.

The increase in the amount of money was, according to Corrado (2000), due to the amount of unregulated funding that flowed through the systems. In order to preserve or increase their power, candidates for the federal and presidential elections raised money for themselves and their political mates. Party committees were the main beneficiaries of this approach and, consequently, played a much larger role in the campaigning than in previous elections.

The regulations of the Federal Election Campaign Act (FECA) were widely undermined or circumvented. The spending of soft money[130] which is not

---

[130] The term "hard money" refers to money that is being raised and spent in accordance with federal restrictions under the FECA. "Soft money", on the other hand, refers to the money that parties can raise for building up the party and for activities that are not defined as "campaign expenditures" under the law. There are no restrictions for soft money when it comes to the size or source of the funding.

subject to the rules of the FECA has been used in many previous elections. These tactics include, but are not limited to, the ability of candidates to use alternative political organizations as surrogate campaign committees and the ability to use political groups for candidate-specific advertising campaigns.

A new tactic that evolved for the 2000 election was the excessive use of soft money. This mainly consisted of spending money on issue advertisements on both the Democratic and the Republican side. The parties claimed that these advertisements did not use any of the "key words" such as "vote for" or "vote against" which would make them subject to the FECA regulations. Some previous court decisions had stated that such key words needed to be included in an advertisement in order for federal regulations to be applied. This tactic was first used in the 1996 Presidential elections, but was perfected in 2000, when neither the Department of Justice nor Congress took any action to stop or even deter this type of circumvention. The FECA considered making new rules on soft-money contributions but no new guide-lines or regulations were set in 1998 or 2000.

Consequently, campaign funding changed its nature, and in 2000 it relied on soft-money advertising by parties to supplement the funds that were raised by the candidates themselves. Candidates became more aggressive in fund raising, and ad hoc political committees and issue advertising by organized political groups became more popular since regulatory actions were not taken against these tactics.

Some political groups and party leaders found another lucrative way to circumvent the FECA restrictions and the disclosure of income sources: Section 527 of the Internal Revenue Code[131]. This section exempts political organizations from income taxes. If an organization does not openly advise voting for or against a certain federal candidate, its actions and activities can seek to "influence the outcome of federal elections" without having to comply with FECA rules and restrictions. In addition, because they ARE exempt from federal taxation, it is legal for them to receive more than $10,000 without being subject to federal gift tax.

When Section 527 became law, Congress assumed that all contributors would already be subject to the FECA, and therefore, they made them exempt from the disclosure regulation. However, this rule makes it virtually impossible to gather information on the contributions of certain groups

---

[131] For further information on Section 527, go to the IRS homepage and look under http://www.irs.gov/newsroom/article/0,,id=103480,00.html

including organizations of the Religious Right. As Rozell (2002) states, the Religious Right was almost invisible in campaign ads in the 2000 election; however, that does not mean that money from these organizations did not find its way into the Bush campaign. According to Wilcox, Religious Right Political Action Committees (PACs) were more active than in the previous elections. Gary Bauer's Campaign for Working Family's made contributions to several candidates with $2.7 million in total receipts.

3.2.2. The Primaries

A presidential campaign starts with the growth of campaign resources. In 1996, seventeen major candidates raised approximately $243 million. In 2000, eighteen candidates raised about $100 million more: $343 million. While the two major Democratic candidates, Al Gore and Bill Bradley, stayed within the somewhat normal range of funds and accepted public funding (which in return meant a cap on the amount that they can raise), the two major Republican candidates, George W. Bush and Steve Forbes, lopsided the battle by foregoing public monies and, thus, freeing themselves from those spending limits.

Bradley, Gore and, in addition, John McCain, a strong advocate for campaign finance reform, used public money for their campaigning. However, the involvement of public money in this presidential prenomination campaign only amounted to about 17%[132], the smallest share ever since the program had been established. This low rate was primarily due to the fact that two of the most predominant candidates passed on participating in the program.

---

[132] The normal share of public funding in a presidential prenomination campaign amounts to approximately 30 percent (Corrado 2000).

Third Chapter: The Campaign

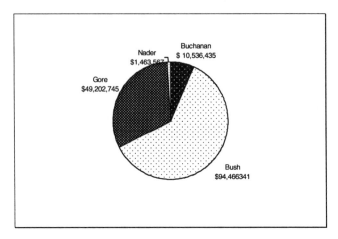

Table 3.1: Adjusted receipts of received donations by candidate in relation to each other.

The following table is adopted from the Federal Election Commission from July 31st, 2000. It describes the presidential prenomination campaigns of the 2000 presidential elections.

Third Chapter: The Campaign

Financial Activity of Presidential Pre-nomination Campaigns in 2000
Table 2: Election and Finances

Candidate	Adjusted Receipts $	Individual Contributions $	Public Matching Funds $	Political Committee Contributions $	Other Receipts $	Total Expenditures $
Democrats						
Gore	49,202,745	33,871,206	15,317,872	0	13,667	42,478,461
Bradley	42,142,565	29,270,589	12,462,045	0	409,931	41,088,547
LaRouche	4,505,658	3,319,038	1,184,372	590	1,658	4,481,792
Republicans						
Bush	94,466341	91,331,951	0	1,960,060	1,174,330	89,135,337
Alexander	3,085,631	2,301,747	0	80,383	703,501	3,085,632
Bauer	12,136,548	7,553,317	4,632,803	6,000	(55,572)	11,761,561
Dole	5,127,832	5,001,635	0	118,292	7,905	5,122,723
Forbes	48,144,976	5,752,150	0	0	42,392,826	47,846,044
Hatch	2,552,723	2,124,707	0	173,016	255,000	2,509154
Candidate	Adjusted Receipts $	Individual Contributions $	Public Matching Funds $	Political Committee Contributions $	Other Receipts $	Total Expenditures $
Kasich	3,191,083	1,702,668	0	77,224	1,411,191	2,335,793
Keyes	10,999,752	7,663,243	3,325,340	10,100	1,057	10,575,767

Third Chapter: The Campaign

McCain	45,047,937	28,143,613	14,467,788	405,599	2,030,937	44,614,846
Quayle	6,317,695	4,083,201	2,087,748	43,200	103,546	5,922,577
Smith	1,614,198	1,522,128	0	17,070	75,000	1,795,231
Other Parties						
Buchanan	10,536,435	6,651,221	3,852,257	1,000	31,967	10,625,582
Hagelin	1,179,980	755,319	314,135	0	110,526	770,257
Nader	1,463,567	1,319,434	100,000	0	44,133	993,506
Browne	1,248,198	66,460,833	0	0	31,000	1,254,213
Subtotals						
Democrats	95,850,968	66,460,833	28,964,289	590	425,256	88,048,800
Republicans	232,684,716	157,180,370	24,513,679	2,890,944	48,099,723	224,704,665
Others	14,428,180	9,943,172	4,266,382	1,000	217,626	13,647,616
Grand Total	**342,963,864**	**233,584,375**	**57,744,350**	**2,892534**	**48,742,605**	**326,401,081**

Note that Pat Buchanan, who first ran on the ticket of the Republican Party but then switched to the Independent Party, still raised a substantial amount of money. He was the candidate with the closest views to the Religious Right which gave him a big advantage over the other independent candidates. In fact, he raised about 2.5 times as much as the other three Independent candidates combined, including Nader. His funds were, however, mainly made up of individual contributions ($6,651,221) and public matching funds ($3,852,247). He got only $1,000 from Political Committee Contributions. This leads us to the conclusion that his campaign was much less organized and that the larger organizations of the Religious Right did not get involved with his campaign. His funds were mainly donations from individual contributors.

In 2000, Bush demonstrated that it was indeed possible to launch a fundraising campaign independent of public funds and, therefore, independent of spending limits. No other major party nominee had ever been successful with this approach. During the primary season, Bush raised over $90 million, more than $25 million more than the total individual receipts of his ten opponents combined. McCain and Forbes both raised about half of what Bush raised; however, the massive contributions towards Bush's campaign made it impossible for the other candidates with smaller budgets to compete.

Although it had been unheard of that an exclusively privately funded candidate would win his party's presidential mantle, Bush did not risk that his campaign would go under-funded. The opposite held true: He wanted to forego public funds in order to be able to spend more.

His fund-raising base was comparable to an incumbent president. This was partly due to the fact that his father's presidency had ended only one and a half terms (or six years) before he entered the race for the presidential nomination himself. In January 1998, more than two and a half years before the actual election, Bush began meeting in Texas with some of the most influential Republican fund-raisers and several other governors who promised to support Bush in his campaign. The Bush family Christmas card list contains over 35,000 entries of people who were sure to support a campaign run by one of the family's sons. In addition to this list, George H. W. Bush's donation network included about 50,000 donors just waiting to be tapped for further funding.

The candidate's own home state showed some promising possibilities as well: The two times that Bush ran for governor of Texas, he generated approximately $41 million. Texas appeared to be well suited to be an additional major contributor.

Third Chapter: The Campaign

In order to make the most of his fund raising potential, Bush used the snowball-system to make sure donations would keep flowing into his "war chest", as he liked to call it. He recruited a group of fundraisers who each pledged to raise approximately $100,000 by finding ten people who were willing to donate $1,000 each. Furthermore, these ten people would be responsible for finding an additional 10 people (Isikoff 2000: 48). By March 2000, Bush had recruited more than 180 pioneers who had raised approximately $18 million.

The success of his campaign exceeded the expectations of the Bush campaign group itself. It also made it clear to the public and the Republican Party that Bush was establishing himself as the front runner, even before any votes had been cast. Right after Bush's announcement that he had put together a presidential exploratory committee, the donations started to pour in. He collected more than twice the amount of money of any of his competitors in the first month alone, $7.6 million. What is remarkable about this sum, besides its size, is that 500 of the donations making up this amount reached the maximum $1,000. The funds continued to grow, and by September 1999 his "war chest" held $57 million where more than $12 million came from Texan residents. His strongest competitors Forbes and McCain had raised far less than these astonishing numbers: Forbes had raised $21 million and McCain[133] had raised less than $9 million. By December, Bush was at $67 million, more than twice as much as any other presidential candidate had ever raised in a pre-elections year (Van Natta 2000). This sum was also more than three times the goal that Bush had set for

himself at this point in time.The clearer it became that Bush would win the fund raising race at such a remarkable gap, the more donors concentrated their efforts on the Bush campaign. At the end of 1999 the Bush campaign stated that they had 171,000 donors and that for every dollar that was raised actively, another 2 dollars came in unexpectedly. Although Forbes poured $28 million of his own money into his campaign, he was unable to stay competitive. He raised about half of what Bush raised. McCain had a total of $16 million where $2 million came as a transfer from his Senate campaign fund.

---

[133] Although the internet increased its importance as a fund raising tool from the 1996 elections, it was not the Bush campaign that made the most of this tool. McCain raised a total of $5 million over the internet and beat out the other candidates in Internet usage.

Third Chapter: The Campaign

The fact that Bush was leading by so much in the fundraising race had a great influence on the continuation of the Republican competition. He was able to build a very sophisticated national campaign infrastructure and spend large sums of money on voter outreach and media leading up to the Iowa caucuses and the New Hampshire primary. At the beginning of 2000, there were 174 paid staff members (in comparison, his most serious competitor had only 80) and 34 local offices in the US. McCain only had 10 offices at that point.

Bush spent as much in the last three months of 1999, $17 million, as McCain had raised throughout the entire year. During the month of February, Bush spent about $400,000 a DAY, adding up to about $13 million total, on television and radio advertising in seven March primary states.

The vastness of Bush's funds and his lead in the polls made it very difficult for the other candidates to even get their campaigns started. There was a feeling of inevitability among the other competitors which in turn lead to even weaker turn outs for their fund raising efforts. In other elections, the Iowa caucuses and the New Hampshire primaries were the point at which the field of candidates thinned out. In this election, by October 1999 six of the Republican candidates had already pulled out of the race.

3.2.3. The Presidential General Election

With Bush and Gore in place as the main candidates essentially by March, the official nomination process from their parties became just a formal procedure. They both accepted public funds for their General Election Campaign which amounted to 67.7 million in public money. They were also allowed to raise private contributions which were subject to federal contribution limits. These contributions were allowed to go towards legal and accounting costs that were related to the federal fund-raising regulations. By the end of this certain type of fund raising, which is known as the General Election Legal and Accounting Compliance (GELAC) fund, both candidates had a total of about $75 million available which was subject to the FECA regulations.

The two other candidates that were able to raise substantial amounts of money were running on minor party tickets: Ralph Nader, who was the Green Party nominee, did not receive any public funding because his party

Third Chapter: The Campaign

did not made the 5% mark in the 1996 elections which is a prerequisite for this type of public financing. Therefore, he was allowed to raise funds on his own with no raising or spending limits in place. Due to his outsider image, he was quite successful at raising money, and by the end of his campaign, he had collected $3.3 million in individual donations.

The Reform Party, with its candidate Pat Buchanan, did indeed qualify for public funding since its 1996 candidate, Ross Perot, received about 8.4% of the total national vote. Therefore, in the end, $12.6 million was awarded to Pat Buchanan's campaign[134]. He would have been allowed to raise up to $67.6 million total; however, he only raised about $600,000 by the time the elections were taking place. Due to the poor number of votes he received, he also left the Reform Party ineligible for pre-election public funding in 2004.

Table 3   Presidential Candidates' General Election Funding (in millions)

Source	Total	Bush	Gore	Buchanan	Nader
Public Funding	$148.8	$67.6	$67.6	$12.6	0.0
Private Contributions	$ 3.9	0.0	0.0	$0.6	$3.3
GELAC Funds	$15.0	$6.8	$8.2	0.0	0.0
Total	$166.7	$74.4	$75.8	$13.2	$3.3

Source: Federal Election Commission, as of November 30, 2000 filings.

---

[134] During the campaign, there was a dispute between Buchanan and the conservative former Natural Law Party's presidential nominee in 1992 and 1996, John Hagelin, since they were both claiming the Reform Party mantle. For the first time, the FECA was forced to decide between two candidates. In mid-September of 2000, the FECA decided to give the money to Buchanan since he was on the ballot in 12 states while Hagelin was only on the ballot in three states. The guidelines require a candidate to be on the ballot in at least 10 states.

Third Chapter: The Campaign

While public funding to the major party candidates remained important in this election, tens of millions of dollars were entered into the race by parties and organized groups during the "hot phase" from summer to Election Day. For the first time, party committees poured more into the campaign than the candidates themselves. For example, the Bush campaign spent $39.2 million on television advertising, about 58% of its public funding. In addition, the Republican National Committee spent $44.7 million. The Gore campaign spent $27.9 million while the Democratic National Committee spent $35.1 million. These figures do not include ads by issue groups that pushed issues clearly aimed at one of the two major party candidates. This makes it clear that the FECA rules need a major overhauling if they are going to be able to put a cap on spending at all[135].

It is difficult to assess how much of an outcome these spending patterns had on the elections. However, due to the stronger and stronger influence of soft money, it is easier for issue or advocacy groups to donate for a certain cause without having to reveal how much they are spending or who is behind these groups.

---

[135] The McCain-Feingold Bill, which was a first step towards campaign finance reform, passed in the senate in April 2001. It was harshly opposed by the Religious Right. Its effects will be seen in the 2004 election cycle.

3.3. Media and the 2000 Election

Christian fundamentalists have traditionally been associated with being somewhat "backwards oriented". While that may hold true for certain cultural values, it certainly does not apply when it comes to the utilization of the media. In this sub-chapter I will give an overview of the structures that members of the Religious Right use in order to get their message out. In addition, I will show how media presentation helped to paint an image of George W. Bush which was favorable to his success.

3.3.1. Religious Right Usage of the Media

The Religious Right has been judged by its resistance, rather than by its enthusiasm, to modernism for many years, especially when it comes to influencing public policy making through their version of voter education. However, when we generally look at the utilization of media by conservative religious institutions, and the Religious Right in particular, in the United States today we find that there is a broad use of all modes of media technology. The last two decades, along with the professionalization of the movement in general, have given way to a very sophisticated approach to utilizing different forms of media. There are hardly any Religious Right organizations, even if they are very small, that do not have their own internet site which, in general, are very well designed and a far cry from simplistic. Since the mainstream media is perceived as being hostile to the Religious Right[163], many institutions of the Religious Right have built their own infrastructure that is complex and diverse when it comes to the types of programs that are being shown to the audience.

---

[163] See also Dobson's comments on the ABC report on Focus on the Family in 2.3.3.

Third Chapter: The Campaign

Berlet (1998) talks about the different types of media that the Religious Right employs:

"The increased use of electronic alternative media in the 1980s and 1990s involved online computer systems, networks, and services; fax networks and trees; short-wave radio programs; networks of small AM radio stations, with syndicated programs distributed by satellite transmissions or even by mailed audiotapes; home satellite dish reception, providing both TV audio/video programs and separate audio programs; local cable television channels, through which nationally produced videos are sometimes aired; and mail-order video and audiotape distributorships."

Not only do these different types of media provide large amounts of information on their own, they also work to reinforce each other by referring to follow-ups for the reader, listener or viewer that are often outside their own information medium (Lesage 1998). Looking, however, at media empires such as the ones of James Dobson or Pat Robertson and to a lesser degree Phyllis Schlaffly shows that they already cover a wide spectrum of media. They all have a broadcasting program and have published several books, newsletters, news alerts, videotapes, magazines, internet sites or have answered letters by their audience.

Message diffusion takes place through a variety of outlets. It is not only the larger organizations, but also single wealthy congregations, independent production companies, think tanks and political action groups, be it political or seemingly non-political, that shower the interested, and sometimes not so interested, audience with information.

It is to be noted that several of the non-political groups of the Religious Right describe themselves as having a "common sense" view of the world rather than believing or adhering to a certain political ideology. Dobson, for example, makes a point of the fact that he is not propagating a certain political or theological point; however, the views that are being propagated through his media outlets coincide exactly with those of the activist Religious Right and are certainly shared by many conservative Republicans.

Dobson et al. mainly apply their "common sense" views, as they call them, when it comes to role stereotyping. Dobson's books on "How to Raise Boys" or "Dare to Discipline" revolve around instilling character in boys and glorifying the stereotypical model of motherhood. As Lesage (1998) notes, these assumptions on roles have concrete political consequences, for example, on the place of women in society or on what homosexuality means for a society.

These "common sense" views often refer to some kind of conspiracy theory where feminists and homosexuals are trying to overtake and/or undermine the traditional family. In these "common sense" views that are being broadcasted or otherwise published, analysis tends to be shallow. A dichotomous view of the world is used to explain processes that are rather complex. However, as they are simple and easy to understand, they are very popular with the audience (Lesage 1998)

3.3.2. Media Distribution via Think Tanks

Since most think tanks in the United States that are included in policy-planning are dependent on massive corporate funding, their political philosophy rarely runs left of the center. For think tanks, such as the Heritage Foundation or the Free Congress Foundation, which is the parent of the National Empowerment Television network, the marketing of their ideas has become a central column of their strategies. As Anna Williams (1998) describes, the director of Heritage Foundation, Edwin Feulner, focuses its mission on getting their ideas out to the public: "We don't just stress credibility, we stress timeliness. We stress an efficient, effective delivery system. Production is one side, marketing is equally important".

Many political organizations, such as the Christian Coalition, rely on the National Empowerment Network (NET) to get information. NET has a top-down organizational and information-delivery style, which assures that the information that the network, or rather the Think Tank behind it, wants to have published will in fact be published.

These Think Tanks have access and maintain contact to a broad base of conservative scholars and policy experts around the nation (Peschek 1987: 33) who are called upon for political commentary whenever media or Congressional hearings demand it. Lesage (1998) describes that the American Enterprise Institute, another conservative Think Tank, runs op-ed pieces in the press, publishes itself and provides the media with political speakers. Among its experts, is Irving Kristol, who, especially in the 2000 Bush administration, was a very close link to the center of political power since he himself belongs to the Neo-conservatives.

Third Chapter: The Campaign

Think Tanks usually have very close contacts to the print media which helps them to influence public opinion. In addition, they are quite successful at placing their employees in policy-making positions by providing "experts" on certain topics. Berlet (1998) suggests that much of the Think Tank research is intellectually shallow; however, due to its simplistic approach, it is a welcome resource for reporters who regularly use it.

The Heritage Foundation has set up its own broadcasting studio in Washington D.C which is often used by conservative talk show hosts who can then address their audience directly from the nation's capital. The Heritage Foundation is also known for writing short and timely papers on public policy which are hand-delivered to congressional staff people. Again, by making information readily available, they increase its usability by a) the congressional staff for whom, if conservative in particular, it means that with relatively little effort, they can provide opinions with some back-up and b) the reporters who will have access to these papers and can easily publish them.

Talk radio plays a very important role in the distribution of informational material. Members and fans of the Religious Right are a very reliable audience which makes talk radio a predictable target for advertisers who can, thus, utilize this predictability in order to dictate advertising fees. In addition, since talk radio like Dobson's or Limbaugh's[164] shows are heard by a mass audience which is only too willing to take cues for political action, it is also an effective and efficient mass mobilizing tool. Since the audience is currently very segmented, the radio host can utilize emotions such as anger, resentment and prejudice. Due to the seemingly personal approach for each listener, the host appears to be close to the audience. By fighting a common enemy, the audience and the host grow closely together. Balz and Brownstein state:

---

[164] In October 2003, Rush Limbaugh had to resign from his additional job as a football commentator on ESPN just after a few days for making racist comments about an African American football player. While this cost him his job on ESPN he continued broadcasting his talk show. However, a few days later, a former housemaid of his accused him of buying thousands of illegal medication pills from her over the years of her employment. Since he had been demanding for years that anybody who buys and/or takes illegal drugs should go to prison, it will be interesting to see what his trial outcome will be. His talk show has been suspended for now.

"The affinity between host and audience made talk radio a mobilizing tool of great power. It stoked anger, sharpened resentments, personalized policy disputes, and clarified issues in a manner that reduced the middle ground" (1996: 189).

Many Religious Right media ventures have either emerged out of a well funded televangelism ministry that takes its funds from donations or the sale of their own products, or they are connected to a corporately funded Think Tank in other ways. Although many of these ventures are decentralized and only a minority can be found in Washington D.C.[165], they generally have a broad base of constituents who provide them with the necessary monetary means.

3.3.3. Bush, Gore and the Media

As Hershey (2001) remarks, with the flood of information during an election campaign, the media tends to present each candidate in a so called "media frame". Each frame represents a central organizing idea or story line. Instead of concentrating on an informational bit, the information is packed into a larger context and then presented. Although such a media frame does not encompass the power of all the media presence, it can still prove influential when one candidate's media frame becomes the dominant way of looking at something.

The candidates, accordingly, utilize media frames themselves. In campaign ads, candidates position themselves with topics that are positively connotated and try to position their counter candidates with topics that are negatively connotated. For example, Bush's campaign team e-mailed friendly viewers and asked them to look for any sort of exaggeration that Gore used in any of the television debates (Hershey 2001). By doing so, he emphasized the media frame of Gore being, as he called it, a "serial

---

[165] For some of these ventures, such as Focus on the Family, there is a specific reason for not being present in Washington D.C. They are accentuating the fact that they are withdrawn from the political establishment and that they are the voice of the ordinary citizen. Often they are located in somewhat rural states in opposition to the more urban structures of the East Coast.

exaggerator"[166]. Journalists were prompted to use that media frame and filter everything they reported on Gore through this filter. Gore's image would be tarnished by seeming to be not trustworthy or appealing enough to become president.

In the 2000 election campaign, a few frames created by the media were dominating the media coverage of Al Gore and George Bush. Gore's coverage consisted mainly of two frames: His personality was described as stiff, ambitious and morally and ethically questionable. His strategic approach was characterized as somewhat chaotic and not able to appeal to his Democratic constituents. The two frames dominated the media and made it seem that Gore had to OVERCOME his tactics rather than to have them help him win the election.

Although the media can not make up these frames in their entirety, nobody would believe a frame for George Bush that emphasized on his outstanding intellect and mastery of speech. The media is free to choose which frame they want to focus on. Gore's more positive attributes had a hard time being recognized through the media coverage, at least until the Democratic convention in August, when his well-timed kiss with wife Tipper seemed to turn his image around to some degree.

However, the media frames screen what sort of information will reach the voters. For example, Gore temporarily mistook Iowa for Wisconsin on his post convention riverboat tour down the Mississippi which hardly made any headlines, because it did not fit into the intellectual frame that Gore was being associated with. One can try to imagine what would have happened, had Bush confused the two states. Bush, on the other hand, never got confronted with the clear exaggeration during the first debate when he claimed that his campaign had been outspent by the Gore campaign when, in fact, Bush had outspent Gore 2:1 by Election Day.

---

[166] In this context, the question of whether the Bush administration, and Bush himself, exaggerated information that they had gotten from the Secret Service in order to "sell" their position on going to war with Iraq becomes even more interesting. The question of whether Bush exaggerated or not received relatively little attention in the media, especially when compared to the Lewinsky scandal. It certainly receives much less coverage than in the European media. Considering the fact that the lack of trustworthiness was one of the major points that Bush tried to criticize Gore for, it is quite amazing that there is no more talk about this particular character trait at this point in time.

Generally, it can be said that issue and policy information was available in the print media prior to the election. The closer the election came, however, the more the media concentrated on the polls, on personality traits of the candidates and on strategic decisions the campaign managers made. This especially holds true for the broadcasting media (Hershey 2001: 70).

While these topics are certainly interesting, it is not clear how much the debate about whether a certain candidate's chance of winning an election should actually influence which candidate would make a better president. In addition, the coverage that was provided through the personality frames was not aimed at characteristics such as experience, management skills or knowledge of world politics. It mainly consisted of such traits as "stiff", "boring" or "self-confident", which, as Hershey writes, might be helpful for the entertainment industry, but not for a future president.

This type of coverage helps broadcasting stations gain more viewers which, consequently, results in higher profits for those involved and maybe even keeps people from staying at home on Election Day. It makes it difficult, however, for each citizen to be armed with the knowledge to make an educated decision in the voting booth.

3.4. Which Candidates Were of Interest to the Religious Right?

3.4.1. Leading up to the Primaries

Early on in the presidential primaries for the 2000 Campaign, the Religious Right was lacking a unifying figure who could collect support from the different factions of the movement. Gary Bauer and Patrick Buchanan, two long standing and very active members of the Religious Right movement, were involved in the early race. Buchanan left the GOP in order to run on the ticket of the reform party while Gary Bauer, much more involved in the Washington lobbies than Buchanan because of his presidency at the Family Research Council, stayed with the GOP but dropped out of the race after a disappointing result of 1% in the New Hampshire Primary.

Steve Forbes had been building alliances with the social conservatives after his failed attempt in the 1996 presidential campaign. Many of these alliances were now involved in his new campaign; however, Forbes dropped out of the campaign along with Bauer when it became clear that the race would be a race between the Arizona Governor, John McCain, and the Texas Governor, George W. Bush.

John McCain had a very long, conservative voting record in his 18 years in Washington and was an avid pro-life voter. In addition, he had a military career where he was a decorated war hero. Whether his views were conservative or not was beyond doubt; however, as James Dobson pointed out, McCain committed adultery earlier on in life and eventually got a divorce from his first wife.

George W. Bush's views on abortion and social issues were almost identical to those of McCain; however, early on in the campaign, Robertson and Reed both supported Bush which was not necessarily a clear indicator for where the rest of the Religious Right was standing, but one can speculate about what Robertson and Reed's motives were. Reed was hired by Bush as his political consultant which gave him prestige and monetary compensation and possibly the hope for a role in the administration to come if Bush were to win.

In addition, Robertson's choice was seen by many analysts to be a practical one (Wilcox 2002: 110). It is quite possible that Bush seemed to be the only candidate that could actually beat Al Gore which, after the years of the Clinton scandals, was crucial to many leaders of the Religious Right. In addition to these practical considerations, many leaders of the Religious

Right believe a nation will be judged by its leaders. By Religious Right standards, the judgment that Clinton would receive could only bring catastrophic results to the nation. Being part of the political establishment and yet emphasizing his religious convictions, Bush seemed to be the candidate that could unite most of the GOP constituency. Wilcox argues that Bush had already convinced numerous leaders of the Religious Right to support him early on in the campaign, even before it had become evident that it would be a race between McCain and Bush. After already giving a pledge to Bush for supporting them, many of these leaders might have been reluctant to "switch teams" in order to support McCain.

Furthermore, the Religious Right attacked McCain for numerous issues. McCain suggested making the language of the GOP more inclusive which would have meant softening the party's anti-abortion platform plank. This was not supported by many of the people in the Religious Right, for whom the strong opposition to abortion was one of the main reasons to become involved in politics in the first place.

McCain switched his opinion on fetal tissue research, which provides a promising approach for the treatment of Parkinson's disease, due to the fact that one of his close friends developed the disease. The Religious Right strongly opposes such research.

He also argued that if his daughter were pregnant, he would leave the decision about having an abortion up to her. This was reported by the media in combination with a statement that he would not support a repeal of the Roe vs. Wade decision. He retracted the latter statement, claiming that he simply misspoke on the subject.

Furthermore, McCain was a strong advocate for the campaign financing reform. Many of the organizations of the Religious Right, such as the Christian Coalition and the National Right to Life Committee who would play a major part in attacking McCain later on in the campaign, were relying on the use of independent expenditure in elections. McCain's reforms would force these organizations to find new ways to finance themselves. In other words, these reforms posed a major threat to the viability of these groups and would be another blow to the Christian Coalition in particular who was already struck with financial problems (Rozell 2002).

The National Right to Life Committee which had given McCain nearly 100% on scorecards in previous campaigns, suddenly sent out mailings to registered GOP voters in South Carolina with photos of a baby on the front

Third Chapter: The Campaign

page and the slogan "This little guy wants you to vote for George Bush" beneath it. For the Michigan primary, Pat Robertson recorded a phone message that was sent out to conservative voters. It included such harsh rhetoric[167], that it made national headlines. The tactics of the Religious Right and Robertson specifically were later asked to tone down their attacks by the Bush campaign (Rozell 2001: 11).

3.4.2. The Primary in New Hampshire

McCain won the first primary in New Hampshire 49% to 30% (Wilcox 2002). The Republicans were not the only ones surprised. Further analysis showed that McCain primarily won because of Independent and Democratic voters. Bush, on the other hand, was the strongest with the Religious Right which did not have a large constituency in the New England states. The analysis of just the Republican constituency showed that Bush won 41% of the votes over McCain's 38%. McCain's supporters came from all wings of the Republican Party and from Independents and Democrats while Bush drew his main votes from the strongly conservative faction of the Republicans.

These were promising results for Bush since the next primary would be in the traditionally more conservative southern state, South Carolina. Fearing the campaign finance reform, Robertson got heavily involved in this primary and led the Religious Right on an attack against McCain which became very personal at times. Robertson, Jerry Falwell and James Dobson shared the opinion that McCain was ill-suited for becoming the Republican candidate, and they worked together to stop his campaign in South Carolina (Rozell, ibid.). Robertson threatened the Republican Party by making comments about how the social conservatives would rather sit out this election than vote for McCain if he should win the primaries. Dobson had already made it clear that he would do anything he could to leave the Republican Party and take as many social conservatives as he could with him if the GOP would not adhere to his rules.

The National Right to Life Committee did the grass-roots campaigning by sending out mass mailings. The fact that the Christian Coalition remained relatively silent in the South Carolina Primary shows the fact that it was

---

[167] See Chapter 2.3.

Third Chapter: The Campaign

very weak, but still the influence of socially conservative voters had not vanished. The National Right to Life Committee picked up these voters and used them for their own purposes.

Robertson, on the other hand, was frequently on television and radio where he made his opinion clear that he found McCain unsuitable for the candidacy.

McCain fought back by heavily criticizing Bush's appearance at Bob Jones University. The university's views on interracial dating and Catholicism were widely known, since the Catholic Church was being described as a "satanic counterfeit" on their website. The founder, Bob Jones, was famous for his derogatory comments on the pope and described Catholicism as a "satanic cult". It was common practice for GOP candidates to speak at Bob Jones University, and therefore, Bush was surprised when McCain publicly criticized Bush's appearance at that university. This time it was McCain who put religion in the middle and used it to benefit his campaign.

However, Bush defended his speech. As soon as polls were showing that he was losing ground with the Catholic constituency, Bush wrote a letter to the former Cardinal, John O'Connor, of New York in which he apologized for his un-meditated appearance at a place where anti-Catholicism and racism were so prevalent.

After Bauer dropped out of the race, the McCain campaign worked hard to get Gary Bauer's endorsement. An endorsement that, in the end, cost Bauer his job with the Family Research Council as many leaders of the Religious Right were not pleased to see this action taking place (Rozell 2002).

3.4.3. The South Carolina Primary

For the South Carolina primary, McCain tried to put religion at the center of his campaigning. For the endorsement by Gary Bauer, the McCain campaign scheduled an appearance at the University of Greenville making sure that the press knew that there would be a major endorsement. Republican, Lindsay Graham (R-S.C.), introduced McCain and implied in her speech that McCain was executing God's will by running for the presidency. In her introduction, McCain played the part of God's tool that was supposed to heal the country with his presidency:

"God has placed John McCain here for a reason, in the right spot at the right time. We have in our midst a man who can heal the wounds of the nation. Really, he shouldn't be alive...John McCain was supposed to die, but he didn't."

Bush normally utilized images that can be created around biblical images, but for McCain this was a rather new approach. Since Bauer was the one endorsing McCain, the allusion to divinity and the Bible at the event were no surprise. McCain's initial strategy was to win over the Religious Right, an attempt that generally failed. Not only did McCain not improve in the polls with the Religious Right, but Bauer lost his credibility with the movement as well and fell behind[168].

South Carolina, a state in which the Religious Right has been traditionally strong, was not to be won in the primaries without the vote of the Religious Right. Bush won South Carolina with the help of the Religious Right 53% to 42%. The voters who did not describe themselves as members of the Religious Right (61%) voted pro McCain 52% to 46%; however, among the voters that described themselves as belonging to the Religious Right, Bush won 68% to 24%. Among voters who stated that abortion should be legal under no circumstances, Bush won 67% to 19%, while McCain won among the 39% of the constituency that stated they were pro-choice.

3.4.4. Michigan

Michigan has a large Catholic population which McCain hoped to mobilize for his campaign. The speech at Bob Jones University hurt Bush's standing with the Catholics, and McCain especially targeted the Catholic voters. However, the Religious Right became very involved in the state's race for the candidacy of the Republican Party.

Michigan is home to the Michigan Right to Life Committee, one of the most powerful Religious Right organizations in the United States[169]. The committee mobilized resources and sent out pro-Bush, anti-McCain

---

[168] Shortly after the end of his campaign Bauer returned to the "Campaign for Working Families" which he founded in 1996. It had been dormant until he returned, and he is currently the chairman. It is not by far the influential role Bauer had as the head of the Family Research Council. According to People for the American Way, FRC has a yearly budget of $10 million while CWF has a yearly budget of about $800,000.
[169] See Chapter 4.2.4. for further information on the NRLC or go to www.NRLC.org

Third Chapter: The Campaign

mailings; 400,000 messages with a smiling baby on the front and "George W. Bush, a Pro-life Vote". The statement that was carried on the inside made positive remarks about Bush's positions on socials issues as well as negative remarks on McCain's alleged views which were "backed" by the fact that McCain had done well in New Hampshire among pro-choice voters.

As mentioned above, Pat Robertson of the Christian Coalition targeted social conservative voters in Michigan by taping and delivering a phone message. In this message, McCain's New Hampshire campaign manager Warren Rudman was denounced as a "vicious bigot" who had made negative comments about the Religious Right. Rudman's point of view on potential presidential candidate, Colin Powell, was not popular with the Religious Right which would not have supported such a candidacy due to Powell's pro-life record. Rudman publicly criticized the Religious Right for its opposition to such a candidacy. Robertson had to back off of his accusation later on and stated "I may have gone on that phrase a little too far" ("Who's a Bigot?", Washington Post, February 24, 2000, p. A20).

In the end, McCain won Michigan 51% to 43% with practically the same voter pattern as in the former primaries. 60% of the voters who were not members of the Religious Right voted for McCain while 36% voted for Bush. Among the Religious Right voters, Bush won easily 66% to 25%. In addition, Democrats (since Michigan was open for votes of non Republican members) [170] voted heavily for McCain; however, McCain would not be able to win the November election with votes that were going to the Democratic Party.

3.4.5. Virginia

Virginia is a state that is similar to Michigan with an "open" primary voting system. However, in order to counteract McCain's strength within voters of the Democratic party, the state GOP leaders who supported Bush introduced a new system. Everyone voting in the GOP primary in Virginia had to sign a so called "loyalty oath". With this oath, the signing party was stating that they would vote for the same person again in the November election. This oath was legally non-binding; however, the system was not explained very clearly, and many of the non-republican voters thought that they had to

---

[170] Some of the States in the United States hold "open" primaries which means that members and non-members of a political party alike can vote in the primaries. However, others hold "closed" primaries where only registered members of a political party get to vote.

somehow follow through with their oath in the November election (Rozell 2001). The turn out with non-Republican voters was much weaker than in the other "open" states.

Virginia, the home of the Christian Coalition and the former Moral Majority, was one of the prime states for the Religious Right. Initially, it did not even seem like McCain was going to be a competitor for Bush; however, shortly before the primary, the distance in the polls between Bush and McCain had shrunk to a single digit percentage with Bush in the lead. Bush had been campaigning

heavily in this state with mass mailings and television ads while McCain had not done anything in that direction.

Shortly before the primary, McCain went to Virginia Beach which is the home town of Pat Robertson. He made a speech that was heavily criticizing the founder of the Moral Majority, Jerry Falwell. McCain clearly distinguished between some Religious Right leaders and the Religious Right electorate; however, few of these distinctions were reported in the media. Gary Bauer urged McCain to also draw a clear distinction between some admired leaders of the Religious Right such as James Dobson, as opposed to Robertson and Falwell; however, the majority of the reports about the speech concentrated on the attacks and failed to show that McCain did not address the Religious Right as a whole.

McCain did not gain anything from his speech. He eventually lost Virginia 53% to 44% to Bush, with the self-identified Religious Right supporting Bush 80% to 14%. 86% of the electorate declared themselves members of the Religious Right; however, among the people that did not belong to the Religious Right, McCain won 52% to 45% (Rozell 2002).

The strategy had not paid off in Virginia; however, one can assume that McCain made the attacks for the benefit of some upcoming primaries that were being held in states that were more progressive. After Virginia was lost, McCain gave an interview on his campaign bus in which he called Robertson and Falwell "evil"[171]. Later on, he back-tracked his statement, but after this message, McCain lost many of the states on Super Tuesday[172].

---

[171] One third of all voters in New York and Ohio said that his "evil" comment had influenced their voting decisions
(http://cnn.com/ELECTION/2000/primaries/NH/results.html).
[172] In Tennessee, the Religious Right made up 27% of the electorate, and in West Virginia they made up 31% of the electorate.

Bauer took back his endorsement and the Religious Right increased their attempt to defeat McCain. The Right to Life Committee alone spent over $500,000 which was more than half of its total spending on all races in the 1998 election cycle.

3.4.6. Conclusion

Even without the comments that ended McCain's campaign, the influence of the Religious Right on the outcome of these primaries was tremendous. By delivering key states to Bush, the Religious Right was the "kingmaker" as Rozell (2001) puts it.

In the general elections in November, the Religious Right constituted about 14% of the voters (Wilcox 2003: 119), a number that is larger than that of participating African American voters and about as strong as that of union members. The movement was not as potent when it came to distributing voter guides although the Christian Coalition claimed they distributed 70 million. TV spots by the Religious Right were basically non-existent, but some radio shows made targeted campaigns by talking to certain candidates, mentioning names and stressing certain issues.

According to the American National Election Studies, a decline of 3% of the votes from the Religious Right occurred in the general elections between the 1996 and the 2000 elections. Despite this decline and given the narrow outcome of the election and the fact that the popular vote went to Al Gore, the remaining 14% of the electorate made a difference.

Third Chapter: The Campaign

3.5. The Image George W. Bush Draws of Himself

3.5.1. Bush Presenting Himself in Front of the Media

George W. Bush has a long history of close relationships to members of the Religious Right, and caters much of his speeches and public appearances to them. In, what USA Today calls, a "carefully crafted strategy" (USA Today, 07-27-2000, 12A), Bush has been courting and is continuing to court the Religious Right on a regular basis. The emphasis he has put on his "born again" experience, has reformed him in the eyes of many to a renewed and repenting Christian who has left his sinful ways behind him.

After winning the nomination of the GOP, Bush declared June 10 to be "Jesus Day" in Texas (Wilcox 2002). His statement read:

> "Throughout the world, people of all religions recognize Jesus Christ as an example of love, compassion, sacrifice and service. Reaching out to the poor, the suffering and the marginalized, he provided moral leadership that continues to inspire countless men, women and children today. To honor his life and teachings, Christians of all races and denominations have joined together to designate June 10 as Jesus Day. Jesus Day challenges people to follow Christ's example by performing good works in their communities and neighborhoods."

As the campaigns are widely covered by the media, it is difficult for a candidate to cater specifically to one particular voter block. In the case of the Religious Right, it proves to be especially difficult since this block only makes up ¼ of the reliable GOP voters, but, on the other hand, it is being eyed by the more moderate force as a hindrance rather than as an asset to the party. Without trying to scare away voters that could possibly be won over by the party's "catch them all" policy, Bush paid tribute to the Religious Right by using highly symbolic language[173] that shows biblical images and generally emphasizes that man was created in the image of God. However, when it comes to stating facts, his position on abortion and homosexuality are generally more inclusive than those of the Religious Right.

---

[173] This symbolic language has been used for years by leaders of the Religious Right in the media. Numerous Televangelists have paved the way for religious topics and linguistic patterns on TV. Although Televengalism is not as dominant anymore as has been in recent years, there are still religious programs that cater to the religious communities. For further reference see: Bretthauer, Berit. *Televengalismus in den USA. Religion zwischen Individualisierung und Vergemeinschaftung.* Campus. Frankfurt/Main, 1999.

As early as 1986, Bush made his "personal recommitment to faith", and in 1988 he gave a speech at the national prayer breakfast. By choosing Dick Cheney, who opposes all abortions he found a running mate that symbolized much of what Bush wants to stand for himself.

Cheney is a man who has a strong faith, who, on the other hand, does not condemn the people that are sinning. "Love the sinner, hate the sin" is a popular motto of Religious Right activists which particularly comes to mind when Bush meets with gay Republicans and declares himself "a better man" afterwards. Consequently, his meeting with these gay Republicans did not raise an outcry by social conservatives in the Republican Party. Bush had already shown them on many occasions that he was a social conservative just as they were. For example, during his time as Governor of Texas, Bush helped defeat a Texan hate-crime bill that would allow homosexuals, in particular, a greater protection from discrimination than before (Boston 2000).

Already when Bush was a governor in Texas, he started talking about more involvement of faith based programs in social services and promoted abstinence vs. birth control, two of the favorite topics of the Religious Right. By doing so he slowly won the trust of evangelicals, and when he signed a legal brief that was encouraging the Supreme Court of Texas to uphold a law which called for prayer before high school games and meets, he cemented that trust which members of the Religious Right had already developed for him (Wilcox 2002).

The speech at Bob Jones University was aimed at the Religious Right electorate as well. While his appearance there sent out a signal of approval to the members of the Religious Right, it certainly fueled his critiques who suspected religious extremism in Bush himself.

The former Christian Coalition executive, Ralph Reed, was hired to be Bush's consultant for the presidential campaign. This also sent a strong signal to the Religious Right, because Reed symbolizes the success of the Christian Coalition. Reed, who had always been more of a politician than a religious activist, is a type of Religious Right figure who goes beyond someone like James Dobson or Pat Robertson. By having Reed help him in his campaign, Bush got a professional politician rather than a Religious Right activist. But he also got someone whose faith apparently plays a great role in his every day life, but who, on the other hand, sees the necessity of trying to achieve something that is actually possible.

George W. Bush, an offspring from the Bush dynasty that is very wealthy and has connected political power and wealth like no other family before them, is trying hard to make himself seem like a "common man". He celebrates his "common sense" approach, as do leaders of the Religious Right, in order to conceil his priveledged and wealthy upbringing. By presenting himself as a sinner and as one of God's children, he makes himself seem humble and as "one of them". As everyone is the same in the eye of God, boundaries between rich and poor are smudged, personal wealth is not a central issue anymore and thus will not be discussed by his constituents. By focussing on topics such as morals, family, faith, and so on he talks about issues that everyone can relate to to some degree. The fact that his personal wealth and social standing are closely connected to his administration and that a large number of members of the administration are also connected to the oil industry is conceiled and hidden from view.

As Bush is emphasizing family values and morals he points towards topics that everyone can understand and somewhat relate to. He can push the values of the Religious Right onto society while declaring that the return to these values will solve social issues. In his presentation, not the system or the distribution of wealth are the reason for many people living in poverty or poor social conditions in the United States, the failure of people to adhere to the moral norms of their forefathers is. Social hirarchies are not being attacked or touched through this approach, the solution is seemingly simple. If everyboday was a good, meaning conservative, Christian, problems would disappear and the government would be needed even less.

Morals and values are also a type of glue that can hold the American society together, as it is culturally and ethnically fragmented. A common denominator that in Bush's opinion should bring the different parts of society together. The place where this "glueing together" usually takes place are the public highschools. However, as ethnic constellations and society are changing, so are the highschools. For this reason, many fundamentalist parents do not want their children subjected to the "glueing process". Not everybody is supposed to adapt to new circumstances a little bit, no, everybody else is supposed to adapt to the christian fundamentalist values.

Bush constructs an image of himself as an evangelical at a time when American society is going through a lot of changes. Globalisation, which to many Americans means that jobs are transferred from the United States to countries that have cheaper labor, presents a threath. Change in general evokes the longing for truths that are unchangable. This need is being fed by the Religious Right, who are refusing to even adapt biblical interpretations to everyday lives.

3.5.2. Bush in Speeches

In his speeches, Bush uses linguistic patterns that are full of biblical references and images. The inauguration speech, therefore, sent a message to the Religious Right, but, on the other hand, it did not appear as overly religious to mainstream Americans. Bush used words such as "spirit", "grace", "faith" in non-religious contexts quite liberally. When thanking Al Gore for being a worthy candidate, he used claims that the campaigns were "a contest conducted with *spirit* and ended with *grace*" (Inaugural Address, January 20, 2001).

He further connects the word "democracy" to the word "faith" and links both of them to the word "creed" which can be understood in a religious or political context. Adding "hope" to it furthers the religious connotation even more.

"Our democratic faith is more than the creed of our country, it is the inborn hope of our humanity" (ibid.)

However, by intertwining these three words with each other, they become religiously connotated and portray Bush in a religious light. Soon thereafter, Bush calls on God, in order to present himself as a humble Christian who answers to a higher spirit:

"I know this is in our reach because we are guided by a power larger than ourselves who creates us equal in His image". (ibid)

At the same time, Bush mentions that according to Christian beliefs we are created equal in God's image, which then raises him up to a higher level. He includes himself in this equally created image in order to receive an almost divine legitimation. Although he appears to recognize the almighty power that God or Jesus Christ present, he takes a piece of that power and attaches it to his own office. By using the image of practically being brought to office by God and constantly reaffirming this status by emphasizing, for example, the daily lecture of the bible, daily prayer and wishing God's blessing on America, he gives the impression that anybody who does not agree with him, does not agree with God. Although he does

Third Chapter: The Campaign

not explicitly mention it, Bush refers indirectly with his remarks to Romans 13[174], which for example played a central point for the propaganda of the "Deutsche Christen" during the Third Reich[175].

In particular, for parts of the Religious Right that hold Romans 13 as one of their key biblical quotes in relation to government, these linguistic patterns evoke a culture of obedience with clear boundaries between good and evil.

In his inaugural speech Bush repeatedly mentioned character building, especially in connection with children and the youth. These statements refer directly to the perception of many of the Religious Right that the U.S. is in a cultural crisis where especially the young people are affected. Again, he refers to God as he mentions that neglected children are not neglected due to God's will. "And whatever our views of its cause, we can agree that children at risk are not at fault. Abandonment and abuse are not acts of God, they are failures of love." (ibid). He also refers to two other key points that the Religious Right has on its agenda: First of all, he mentions the military and defense spending which are too weak in the eyes of the Religious Right. Bush states that he wants to

"build our defenses beyond challenge, lest weakness invite challenge" (Inaugural Speech). By this announcement he implies that he will make America invincible and restore it to its former glory.

---

[174] 1Let every person be subject to the governing authorities. For there is no authority except from God, and those that exist have been instituted by God. 2Therefore he who resists the authorities, resists what God has appointed, and those who resist will incur judgment. 3For rulers are not a terror to good conduct, but to bad. Would you have no fear of him who is in authority? Then do what is good, and you will receive his approval, for he is God's servant for your good. 4But if you do wrong, be afraid, for he does not bear the sword in vain; he is the servant of God to execute his wrath on the wrongdoer.

[175] The "Deutsche Christen" were a group within the church that from 1932 on were pushing for the Nazi program in the church. In the church elections on July 23rd, 1993 they won the majority and took over power in almost all state churches in Germany on September 29th 1933, when their patron Ludwig Mueller became Reichsbishop. Their demands within the church, such as forcing everyone and everything into line, the leadership principle, a.s.o. soon led to the "Kirchenkampf" (battle of the churches). One of the Bible verses that was supposed to give them legitimation for supporting the NSDAP was Romans 13. One of the major opponents of the "Deutsche Christen" were the "Bekennende Kirche" under Martin Niemoeller. See also: Perels, Joachim. „Die Hannoversche Landeskirche im Nationalsozialismus 1935-45. Kritik eines Selbstbildes", *Beiheft Junge Kirche.* H. 9/1995, S. 1-23.

A second key point that he mentions is the "reclaiming of America's schools" which is also a major topic for the Religious Right. According to popular belief within factions of the Religious Right, education has undergone a change that dates back to the cultural revolutions of the 1960's. Furthermore, the only way to prevent more damage, is to take back America's educational institutions and start the "counter-revolution" which will return everything to its pre 60's and sometimes even pre-war or beginning of the 20th century condition.

Furthermore, Bush mentions pastoral prayers which, in his eyes, are sometimes the only way to relieve one's hurt. He then proceeds to quoting a "saint of our times" (ibid). Bush mentions the calling the he is sharing with others to do good and to be a valuable member of society. However, the word "calling" is particularly used within the Religious Right where especially pastors are supposed to hear the "calling" from God to be pastors. Bush plays with his role as the head of civil religion in the United States more so than other presidents. By allusions to the calling that the clergy hear, he reemphasizes his legitimation by God.

At the end of his inauguration speech, Bush mentions that humankind "is not the story's author, who fills time and eternity with his purpose. Yet his purpose is achieved in our duty, and our duty is fulfilled in service to one another." Again, Bush makes himself seem humble and refers to the service he is willing to provide for others. Here, Bush refers to parts of the second greatest commandment given by Jesus in Matthew 22:36-40: Love thy neighbor as yourself.

Concluding his speech, Bush refers to an angel that is still riding in the whirlwind and is directing this storm. He finishes with "God bless you all, and God bless America".

3.5.2.1. Videotaped Remarks to the Christian Coalition Road to Victory

Bush's rhetoric before the election was seemingly less religiously oriented. Even at a speech that he gave for the Christian Coalition, his images did not hold quite as many religious patterns as they tended to have after the election. Again Bush remarked that he wanted to tackle the key issues of the Religious Right: Education, rebuilding the military, sexual abstinence, abortion matters and the building of good character in children. He emphasized exactly what the Religious Right had been discussing for years. Bush openly mentioned the Bible, which he will put his hand on for the oath that he will take "so help me God". In this speech, he did not use allusions to biblical themes and images, but he still mentioned topics that were important to the members of the Religious Right. However, he did not use as much of a visual language as he did in other speeches after his inauguration and in particular after September 11.

Bush presented himself in this speech as a man that is "down to earth" and basically "one of us". He still used figurative language, however, with fewer biblical allusions.

His approach started with feeding the distrust that many of the people that constitute the Religious Right have when it comes to the government in Washington, D.C. According to Minkenberg, the Religious Right consists mainly of people living in the rural areas while the ideologically motivated activists accumulate in Washington D.C. (Minkenberg 1990: 118). Bush emphasizes that he will aim for a government that becomes less intrusive which includes tax regulations. In his speech, he accentuates that the government should respect the values of its citizens. Parents should have more control over what is being taught in the classroom, also an old Religious Right favorite, since they have been against sex education or the teaching of evolution for decades.

Bush points out the fact that Gore has had a long career in Washington, implying that Gore has lost touch with reality by calling on the image of "the spaceship Washington" [176] whose members supposedly are withdrawn from "the little guy" and work only to secure the establishment. Bush certainly does not mention his own role and long career in politics.

Bush refers to Gore as someone that doesn't trust the people he governs which makes him even more withdrawn from the "simple people". In another segment of the speech, Bush mentions the "distant central office" which makes decisions far from the people that are concerned on the local level. Here the image of the "spaceship Washington" is being called upon again. By making the link between Gore and the centralized structure, Bush equates himself with someone that is close to the people who likes decisions to be made on a local level. This point is being emphasized in his speeches over and over again which is supposed to soften the image of the heartless capitalist that the GOP is sometimes associated with. Bush's rhetoric always talks about compassionate conservatism which, in reality, has the same aims. In times when the economy is weak and more and more people

---

[176] The term "Spaceship Washington" refers to the perception of many Americans that the Federal Government is out of contact with the common people's everyday problems.

get laid off, the word "compassion" is supposed to offer comfort and evoke a "warm fuzzy" feeling when it comes to George Bush.

As far as education is concerned, he puts an emphasis on performance evaluations for students, schools and teachers. While also propagating disciplinary action in the classroom in order for children to build character, he also feeds the image of an authorative model of how society should be run. Control seems to be the best approach when it comes to educating children and restoring moral values and character in the younger generation. When talking about restoring discipline and reducing intrusion into the private home by the federal government, he also refers to the ongoing debate about child abuse and how much power the government should have in order to prevent violence against children[177]. Many of those parents feel that their rights are seriously threatened by laws that some states have passed which make corporal punishment illegal.

Bush mentions abortion in this speech as well although he does not speak up against abortion in all cases. He makes the point that he will sign a bill against partial birth abortions[178], but, other than that, he concentrates his argumentation on promoting adoption and parental notification.

Further on in the speech, Bush quotes Ronald Reagan, who was the first president to court evangelicals for an election. Many of the members of the Neoconservatives and the Religious Right served under Reagan. By quoting Reagan, Bush reminded members of the Religious Right of the ties that had been formed between the GOP and the Religious Right ever since then. He again links "the little people" with the politics of the GOP:

"But, as Ronald Reagan said, 'You can't be for big government, big bureaucracy, and still be for the little guy'. Like Ronald Reagan, I believe that the freedom we cherish ultimately depends on the values our families teach." (September 30, 2000, CC Road to Victory Luncheon).

These two sentences have nothing in common with regard to content. They are not connected at all. However, by putting them together, Bush calls upon traditional values and puts as many key words into one sentence as possible. These key words serve as buzz words and make the audience

---

[177] In this context, the books by James Dobson, which are highly popular within the constituents of the Religious Right, come to mind: "Dare to discipline", "Love must be Tough", "Temper Your Child's Tantrums", etc. By mentioning the will to restore discipline at school, he linked himself to James Dobson who is a great influence on the constituents of the Religious Right.

[178] The Senate approved the bill in March 2003, it was signed in October 2003.

Third Chapter: The Campaign

recognize terms that are important to them. Thus, the appeal of the speech is much larger and has a more direct approach than a different terminology would have been able to achieve. Contact between the speaker and the audience is much closer, and it will be easier to convince the listeners that "one of them" is speaking to them. Although analysis of voting behavior for the 2000 election has shown that the participation of evangelical voters who actually voted conservative has declined by two percent from 15.5% to 13.7% (Wilcox in Wayne and Wilcox 2002: 117), the Religious Right is an important voting block.

He ends his speech by promising to hold up the honor and dignity of the office, which is a comment aimed at former President Clinton, one of the favorite enemies of the Religious Right.

3.5.2.2. Speech: A New Prosperity: Seats for All at the Welcome Table

Republican National Convention 2000, Philadelphia, Pennsylvania

In his speech at the 2000 national convention, Bush draws a picture of himself which is strictly aligned with the image of the "compassionate conservative". Regarding the topics of Welfare Reform and Childcare, Bush spent about half the time on faith based initiatives and the value they hold for America. He emphasizes the importance of faith which, in his eyes, makes many of these programs very effective.

Bush puts faith based charitable programs into the role of victims who were severely wronged by the Clinton administration. This is a role that the Religious Right often assumes as well which is aimed for greater sympathy by advertising their so called victimization. At the same time, this image of a victimized group makes the group appear much less threatening, as the strength of the movement stands in contradiction to their role as something that has to be protected.

Already the title "Seats for all at the Welcome Table" is inclusive for most factions of the GOP, but for the Religious Right, it has additional meaning. One of their earliest demands at the beginning of the 1990's was "to get a seat at the table". Ralph Reed propagated that this was all the Religious Right, or more accurately, the Christian Coalition wanted in the beginning.

In the part of his speech in which he refers to faith based initiatives, Bush represents himself as somewhat of a hero who has helped many lives through the help of faith based initiatives[179]. He speaks about the changes that happened in his home state of Texas after implementing charitable choice in welfare. This took place while Bush was governor of Texas; however, he refers to himself as "the governor" and makes the situation more formal than it actually is. By somewhat withdrawing from his own position, he also makes the mentioning of the faith based program in Texas more credible since it does not seem like he is praising his own achievements.

Bush presents himself as a fighter for faith, and allusions to a noble crusader are not a coincidence. He declares that faith based initiatives are basically being black listed because the Clinton administration insisted "that all symbols of religion must be removed or covered over" in order to be eligible for government programs (Party Platform: A New prosperity: Seats for All at the Welcome Table). However, Bush again turns the removal of religious symbols into the linguistic patterns of a victim:

> "They [Religious Organizations with charitable programs] are being treated unfairly just because they will not conceal nor compromise the faith that makes them so effective in changing lives" (ibid.)

Religious Organizations, and, thus, the Religious Right, are being portrayed in Bush's speech as a mild form of a martyr which they have become due to the

fact that they are "upright Christian citizens" who fight for their Christian beliefs without submitting to the "morally inferior" government[180] of the Clinton administration. Bush mentions the faith based programs as 100% positive and as something that has to be supported without any doubt. Although theoretically all faiths could be concerned, the Religious Right is being addressed and the implication of the addressed faith is Christian. In the last line, Bush refers to "individuals created in the image of God", which is foremost Christian terminology and will not be used by other non-Christian faiths.

---

[179] Interestingly enough, he never mentions his own battle with alcohol.
[180] Due to the fact that many Americans were tired of the Lewinsky affair, the impeachment of Clinton and the fact that the Democratic candidate was part of that Clinton administration was not being stressed in particular by the GOP. Rather than to risk being called "obsessed" with the Lewinsky affair once again, the Conservative party restricted itself to using allusions in speeches to express its unhappiness with the outcome of the impeachment process.

Bush calls upon the armies of compassion, another allusion which is connoted with Christian meaning. Again, the image of crusades comes to mind, when armies of Christians entered the Holy Land.

In this speech, Bush massively uses the image of the Christian Crusades, because he is trying to evoke a spirit of renewal and awakening which are also Christian images. He depicts himself as someone who will bring renewal, who will "clean up" the morally corrupt and who will help Christianity get its proper place "at the table". Bush uses keywords that directly appeal to voters whose lives are centered on the bible and who are perceptive to this type of linguistic pattern. He uses these patterns and images throughout his speeches, respectively to a greater or lesser extent. The usage of these patterns seems to be particularly strong when he is speaking to audiences that are not necessarily particularly religious. Many of the key words will be missed by a mainstream audience. Thus, when he is not speaking on topics that hold special meaning to the Religious Right, he still appeals to that group on a meta-linguistic, maybe even a subconscious, level. He presents himself as upright and determined, ready to defend Christianity's "rightful" place in government.

At the end of the speech, Bush emphasizes his belief that "the American people have a long and seasoned history of working wonders". To make wonders happen is a concept that again stems back to the Bible. With this wording, Bush draws an image of the American people where they seem like an army of Gods that are working wonders. He uses the biblical image in order to elevate the American people to something superior. By doing so, Bush expresses his own appreciation of religious faith and the things "God's people" perform within society. He courts the Religious Right and custom tailors many of his speeches towards their needs.

3.5.3. Conclusion

Bush talks frequently about "the poor and those on the margins of society" or "the elderly and sick, the young, the unborn". He puts that into context with his slogan of the "compassionate conservative" who he proclaims he is. However, by focussing on the religious aspects and by encouraging faith based initiatives, he is pulling government out of welfare. By demonstrating his own faith and focussing on family values in the context of social policy, he implies that social problems can be solved by faith based initiatives, and, more importantly, by the return to "proper" Christian morals. This will reduce spending tax money on welfare. On the same hand it ensures that faith based programs can spread their faith and influence among those that are in need of aid. As shown in chapter 3.1.4 community outreach plays a major role in influencing political involvement. However, it can also mean that for people that are not willing to adhere to certain norms of these faith based organizations, such as attending bible study groups or church sponsored events, there might not be a program that is willing to assist them. Faith based organizations become moral enforcers which in this case, also enforce the moral framework that the administration is pushing.

By declaring himself as one of God's children "created in the image of God" (Seats for all at the Welcome Table), he makes himself equal to "the common people", diverting attention from the priveledged life that he is living. As they are all sinners in front of God, wealth becomes a minor concern and moral righteousness is a goal that they can all aim for and that everybody can relate to.

4. Conclusion

Before the presidential campaign of the 2000 elections had even started, political analysts believed that the election would be a close one and that the Religious Right would not have much of an influence. But only one of the predictions came true-that the election would be a close one.

The election was actually much closer than anticipated, and while Bush won the election, Gore won the popular vote, showing the deep split in the voting of the American People.

Since the Religious Right was lacking a candidate who could unify the movement from the offset, it was widely believed that they would not make a significant difference. Numerous candidates tried to appeal to the constituency of the Religious Right. In 1999 Christian social conservative, John Ashcroft, was believed to be the one who large numbers of movement members would vote for. However, when he announced that he would not be running, Gary Bauer, Dan Quayle, Steve Forbes, Pat Buchanan and, last but not least, George Bush started seeking the votes of the Religious Right.

In addition, numerous organizations of the Religious Right faced some set backs. Apart from Focus on the Family, organizations were losing members and, thus, money to operate. As it turned out, this did not mean that people were not voting at the grass-roots level, it just meant that the movement was not as organized as it once was. The Christian Coalition was hit especially hard, and political analysts predicted a waning influence by Pat Robertson.

Robertson and others, such as Dobson, picked their battles carefully. Robertson's strategy of making taped phone calls to "get out the votes" proved to be successful in the states that he chose. Dobson headed the only organization, Focus on the Family, which was still gaining members and listeners. With his threats to the GOP about taking the more conservative constituents with him if he left the party, presidential candidates made sure to include the Religious Right in their campaigning. If Dobson had convinced his listeners to stay at home on election day, it would have meant a different outcome of the election in the end.

The organizations of the Religious Right were considered to be one of their major strengths. Since the Christian Coalition, which was one of the major organizations within the Religious Right, was facing serious troubles prior to the elections, many analysts believed that the Religious Right would not

Conclusion

have much of an influence. Despite its troubles, it still managed to mobilize voters in the GOP primaries on the local level.

Many people believed that the movement purists would rather vote for a candidate who held firm views on issues which were important to the Religious Right instead of for somebody who had a better appeal to a larger group of voters. This held true for some of the former elections when members of the Religious Right were believed to have cost the vote for the GOP. However, in the 2000 election, these purists became seemingly more pragmatic. Although George W. Bush had a social conservative voting record, movement insiders, such as Gary Bauer or Pat Buchanan, would have stood a better chance to become the movement's favorite candidates, since they were compromising less on issues important to the Religious Right.

Pat Robertson, Ralph Reed and James Dobson decided to support George Bush very early on. This did not initially unite the movement, but it sent out a strong signal to the movement's constituents, which gained more and more momentum as time went on.

Their endorsement came at a time when Bush was outspending his closest competitor, John McCain, by large margins and had already gotten endorsed by major party officials. The leadership of the Religious Right realized that Bush would have a good chance at winning the nomination and consequently backed his campaign early on as well. With this move, they were hoping to secure an influential position if George W. Bush were to become President.

George W. Bush started as early as 1999 to make contact with leaders of the Religious Right. He talked to them about his own personal religious experience and the subsequent conversion from an alcoholic party boy to a devout Christian and family man. The sharing of his personal testimony, which plays a major part in evangelical circles, made him a more likely candidate for evangelicals.

After McCain verbally attacked some of the movement's leaders, it was easier for the Religious Right to paint their picture of him as a bigot, rather than to explain that McCain's plans of campaign finance reform would hurt many of the movement's organizations financially.

Conclusion

In addition, it was clear to many of the movement members that they did not want to have somebody from the Clinton administration being in charge for one, potentially two, more terms.

These factors were unique to the 2000 election and do not necessarily indicate that the movement has gained momentum. However, it would be premature to declare that the movement is stagnant. Although its organizations are experiencing financial difficulties, mass mailings, computerized phone calls and other such strategies motivate the voters in the primaries more than ever.

Bush actively sought the votes from the Religious Right. He tailored his speeches and comments to the needs of the movement by entering key words that would appeal to that constituency. Talking about his faith, declaring Jesus Christ as his personal hero and the Bible as his favorite book, he made Religion the center of his campaign aimed at the Religious Right.

George W. Bush won the GOP nomination, because it was handed to him by the Religious Right. According to the exit polls, the Republicans who were also members of the Religious Right outvoted the ones who are not. Although the Religious Right was less active in the general election, 14% (down from 17% in 1996) of all voters still belonged to the movement. That is more than the union vote count or the African American vote count. In an election as close as this one, this percentage becomes even more important.

John Ashcroft being appointed as the Attorney General was the prize the Religious Right was awarded for handing the election to George W. Bush. However, more movement activists received positions: Secretary of Health and Human services, Tommy Thompson and Secretary of Interior, Gale Norton, are two other examples.

One of Bush's first actions when he came into office was to ban U.S. funds to overseas population agencies that also perform abortions. In addition, he ordered a new investigation into the FDA's approval of the abortion pill, RU-487, and signed a bill that prohibited late term abortions.

Although the Religious Right remains a strong player in United States' politics, its influence has not been strong enough to accomplish some of its main goals. Roe vs. Wade remains untouched, although that could be changed by a few new appointments to the Supreme court. Abortions, in general, have only become slightly more difficult to obtain; more women

Conclusion

than ever are working; children's rights have been held up by states signing bills that make corporal punishment illegal; schools are still teaching sex education which does not promote abstinence as the only way to go; and evolution remains on most school district's curricula. In addition, homosexuality has become more accepted, and hate crimes, such as the murder of Matthew Shepard in Wyoming, have been punished severely, sometimes encouraging cities and states to add hate-crime bills to their laws[126].

This does not mean, however, that more success for the Religious Right is impossible in the future. All the issues mentioned above could be affected by the appointment of one or two new judges to the Supreme Court.

The Religious Right continues to be strongly supported by a substantial part of the population. It has become more professionalized and more flexible in its tactics. It is a force to be reckoned with, and since it has unprecedented power and influence within the Bush administration, it is not likely to vanish or have less of an impact in the near future.

---

[126] On October 6th 1998, Matthew Shepard was beaten by Aaron McKinney and Russell Henderson due to the fact that he was gay. They tied him to a fence post out by a country road outside of Laramie, WY and left him lying there. He died 5 days later from his injuries. Among other Religious Right leaders, Pat Robertson and Jerry Falwell were quick to deny any connection between their harshly anti-gay rhetoric and hate-crimes in general. For additional information on the murder, see the memorial page set up by the New York times at: http://www.nytimes.com/ads/marketing/laramie/index.html.

5. Bibliography

Adams, Willi Paul and Peter Lösche (Pbl.). *Länderbericht USA: Geschichte, Politik, Geographie, Wirtschaft, Gesellschaft, Kultur.* Bonn, 1998.

Albrecht, Horst. *Die Religion der Massenmedien.* Kohlhammer. Stuttgart, 1993.

Ammerman, Nancy T. *Congregation and Community.* Rutgers University Press. New Brunswick, 1997.

Ammerman, Nancy T. "North American Protestant Fundamentalism." In: Kintz, Linda and Julia Lesage (eds.). *Media, Culture and the Religious Right.* University of Minnesota Press. Minneapolis, 1998.

Baer, Denise L. and David A. Bositis. *Elite Cadres and Party Coalitions.* Greenwood Press. New York, 1988.

Baer, Denise L. and David A. Bositis. *Politics and Linkage in a Democratic Society.* Prentice Hall. New Jersey, 1993.

Balz, Dan and Ronald Brownstein. *Storming the Gates: Protest Politics and the Rise of the Christian Coalition.* Prometheus Books. Amherst, 1996.

Barret, Laurence I. "Fighting for God and the Right Wing." *Time.* September 13, 1993: 58-60.

Baum, Gregory. *Neo-conservatism: Social and Religious Phenomenon.* The Seabury Press. New York, 1981.

Bealy, Frank W. *The Blackwell Dictionary of Political Science.* Blackwell Publishers. Malden, 1999.

Bellant, Russ. *National Catholic Reporter.* November 18, 1988.

Belloni, Frank P. and Dennis C. Beller. *Faction Politics: Political Parties and Factionalism in Comparative Perspective.* Clio Press. Oxford, 1978.

Benoit, William L. "The Functional Approach to Presidential Television Spots: Acclaiming, Attacking, Defending 1952-2000." *Communication Studies* 52.2 (2001): 109+.

Bentley, Rosalind. "Promise Keepers' grip loosens, but its hold remains". *Minneapolis Star Tribune.* September 6, 2002.

Berlet, Chip. "Who Is Mediating the Storm? Right Wing Alternative Information Networks." In: Kintz, Linda and Julia Lesage (eds.). *Media, Culture and the Religious Right.* University of Minnesota Press. Minneapolis, 1998.

Bible, The. www.bible.com.

Black, Earl and Merle Black. *The Vital South.* Harvard University Press. Cambridge, 1992.

Boelsche, Jochen. "Bush's Masterplan. Der Krieg der aus dem Thinktank kam." *Der Spiegel.* March 4, 2003.

Boston, Rob. "Preachers, Politics and Campaign." *Church & State.* Sept. 2000.

Boston, Rob. "The G.O.P Holy War." *Church & State.* Apr. 2000.

Boston, Robert. *The Most Dangerous Man in America? – Pat Robertson and the Rise of the Christian Coalition.* Prometheus Books. Amherst, 1996.

Boyer, Paul. *When Time Shall Be No More: Prophecy Belief in Modern American Culture.* The Belknap Press of Harvard University Press. Cambridge, 1992.

Bretthauer, Berit. *Televengalismus in den USA. Religion zwischen Individua- lisierung und Vergemeinschaftung.* Campus. Frankfurt/Main, 1999.

Brickner, Bryan W. *The Promise Keepers: Politics and Promises.* Lexington Books. Oxford, 1999.

Brewer, Priscilla J. *Shaker Communities, Shaker Lives.* University Press of New England. Boston, 1988.

Brocker, Manfred. "Die Christliche Rechte in den USA." In: Michael Minkenberg / Willems (eds.). *Politik und Religion.* PVS-Sonderheft 33. 2002: p. 256f.

Brown, Clifford W., Lynda W. Powell, and Clyde Wilcox. *Serious Money: Fundraising and Contributing in Presidential Nomination Campaigns.* Cambridge University Press. Cambridge, 1995.

Bruce, Steve, Peter Kivisto and William H. Swatos, Jr. *The Rapture of Politics.* Transaction Publishers. London, 1995.

Bruce, Steve. *Fundamentalism.* Polity Press. Malden, 2000.

Bruce, Steve. *The Rise and Fall of the New Christian Right: Conservative Protestant Politics in America 1978 – 1988.* Clarendon Press. Oxford, 1988.

Bush, George W. *Inaugural Address.* January 20, 2001.

Bush, George W. quoted in *Christian Science Monitor.* April, 22 1997.

Bush, George W. quoted in *USA Today.* July 27, 2000. pp. 12A.

Bush, George W. *Remarks at the Road to Victory Luncheon.* September 30, 2000, Christian Coalition Annual Road to Victory Luncheon.

Carney, James. "The GOP Mantra: Keep Dobson Happy." *Time Magazine.* May 11, 1998.

Cigler, Allan J. "Interest Groups and Financing the 2000 Elections." In: Maggleby, David B. (ed.). *Financing the 2000 Election.* Brookings Institution Press. Washington, D.C., 2002.

Cohen, Ariel Dr. "Comment." In: http://www.heritage.org/views/2002/ed041802.html

Cohen, Diane and A. Robert Jaeger. *Sacred Places at Risk: New Evidence on How Endangered Older Churches and Synagogues Serve Communities.* Philadelphia: Partners for Sacred Places, 1997.

Conason, Joe. "Ralph Reed, Smart As the Devil." *Commentary.* March 1983: 59 -72.

Conason, Joe. "The Religious Right's Quiet Revival." *The Nation.* April 27, 1992: 551, 553-59.

Conover, Pamela J. and Virginia Gray. *Feminism and the New Right: Conflict over the American Family.* Praeger. New York, 1983.

Conway, M. Margaret, Gertrude Steuernagel and David Ahern. "Women and Political Participation." *Congressional Quarterly Press.* Washington, D.C., 1997.

Cooper, Cynthia L. "Republican Party Donates to Right to Life." http://www.womensenews.org/article.cfm?aid=1259. 2003.

Corrado, Anthony. "Financing the 2000 Elections." In: Pomper, Gerald M. *The Election of 2000.* Seven Bridges Press. New York, 2001.

Corrado, Anthony. "Financing the 2000 Presidential Election." In: Maggleby, David B. (ed.). *Financing the 2000 Election.* Brookings Institution Press. Washington, D.C., 2002.

Bibliography

Diamond, Sara. *Not by Politics Alone: The Enduring Influence of the Religious Right.* The Guilford Press. New York, 1998.

Diamond, Sara. *Roads to Dominion: Right-Wing Movements and Political Power in the United States.* The Guilford Press. New York, 1995.

Diamond, Sara. *Spiritual Warfare: The Politics of the Christian Right.* South End Press. Boston, 1989.

Dionne, E. J. Jr. "The Clinton Enigma: Seeking Consensus, Breeding Discord" In Pomper, Gerald M. *The Election of 2000.* Seven Bridges Press. New York, 2001.

Dionne, E. J. Jr. *Why Americans Hate Politics.* Simon and Schuster. New York, 1991.

Dionne, E. J. Jr. "Robertson's Victory in Ballot Shakes Rivals in G.O.P. Race." *New York Times.* September 14, 1987: B12.

Dixon, A. C., general ed. *The Fundamentals.* Testimony Publishing. Chicago, 1910-1915.

Dobson, Ed and Cal Thomas. *Blinded by Might.* Zondervan. 2nd Edition. Grand Rapids, 2000.

Dobson, James. *The Strong-Willed Child.* Tyndale House. Wheaton, 1982.

Dobson, James. *Bringing Up Boys: Practical Advice and Encouragement for Those Shaping the Next Generation of Men.* Tyndale House. Wheaton, 2001.

Dobson, James. *Dare to Discipline.* Tyndale House. Wheaton, 1974.

Dobson, James. *Life On The Edge: A Young Adult's Guide to a Meaningful Future.* Word Publishing. Dallas, 1995.

Dobson, James. *Letter to his Supporters.* March 1995a.

Dobson, James. *Temper your Child's Tantrums.* Tyndale House. Wheaton, 1986.

Doerr, Edd. "Promise Keepers: Who What and Why?" Vol. 126n, *USA Today Magazine.* March 1, 1998.

Doyle, Rodger. "Why America is Different: Puritans, Circuit Riders, and the Free Market." In: *Free Inquiry.* Volume 22, Issue 3. Summer 2002.

Edsall, Thomas B. "The Cultural Revolution of 1994: Newt Gingrich, the Republican Party, and the Third Great Awakening." In: Byron E Shafer (ed.). *Present Discontents: American Politics in the Very*

Late Twentieth Century. Chatham House Publisher. New Jersey, 1997.

Edsall, Thomas B. and Cici Connolly. "Christian Right-GOP Alliance Crumbling." *Valley News.* March 28, 1999: A1.

Edsall, Thomas B. and David S. Broder. "Robertson accuses Kirk of Bigotry" *Washington Post.* March 2, 1986: A4.

Ersoz, Meryem. *"Gimme that Old-Time Religion."* In: Kintz, Linda and Julia Lesage (eds.). *Media, Culture and the Religious Right.* University of Minnesota Press. Minneapolis, 1998.

Falwell, Jerry, Ed Dobson, et al. (Publishers). *The Fundamentalist Phenomenon. The Resurgence of Conservative Christianity.* Baker Book House: 2nd edition. Grand Rapids, 1986.

Fetscher, Iring (ed). *Neokonservative und "Neue Rechte".* Beck. Muenchen, 1983.

Foot, Kirsten A., and Steven M. Schneider. "Online Action in Campaign 2000: An Exploratory Analysis of the U.S. Political Web Sphere." *Journal of Broadcasting & Electronic Media.* 2002.

Foster, Lawrence. *Women, Family and Utopia: Communal Experiments of the Shakers, the Oneida Community and the Mormons.* Syracuse University Press. Syracuse, 1992.

Freeman, Jo and Victoria Johnson. *Waves of Protest: Social Movements Since the Sixties.* Rowman & Littlefield. Lanham, MD, 1999.

Gardiner, Steven. "Through the Looking Glass and What the Christian Right Found There." In: Kintz, Linda and Julia Lesage (ed). *Media, Culture and the Religious Right.* University of Minnesota Press. Minneapolis, 1998.

Gilbert, Christopher P. and David Peterson. "Minnesota: Christians and Quistians in the GOP." In: Rozell and Wilcox (eds.). *God at the Grassroots: The Christian Right in the 1994 Elections.* Rowman & Littlefield. Lanham, MD, 1998.

Giugni, Marco, Doug McAdam and Charles Tilly. *From Contention to Democracy.* Rowman & Littlefield. Lanham, MD, 1998.

Giugni, Marco. "Social Movements and Change: Incorporation, Transformation, and Democratization." In: Giugni, McAdam and Tilly (eds.). *From Contention to Democracy.* Rowman & Littlefield. Lanham, MD, 1998.

Glaser, James. *Race, Campaign Politics and the Realignment in the South.* Yale University Press. New Haven, CT, 1996.

Glazer, Nathan. "Fundamentalists: A Defensive Offensive." In: Richard John Neuhaus and Michael Cromartie (eds.). *Piety and Politics: Evangelicals and Fundamentalists Confront the World.* Ethics and Public Policy Center. Washington, D.C., 1987: 245-58.

Greeley, Andrew. *Religion Around The World: A Preliminary Report.* Chicago, 1991: p. 39.

Green, John C. "The Christian Right and the 1994 Elections: An Overview." In: Rozell and Wilcox (eds.). *God at the Grassroots.* Rowman & Littlefield. Lanham, 1995.

Green, John C. and James L. Guth. "From Lambs to Sheep: Denominational Change and Political Behavior." In: Leege and Kellstedt (eds.). *Rediscovering the Religious Factor in American Politics.* M. E. Sharpe. New York, 1993.

Green, John C. and James L. Guth. "The Christian Right in the Republican Party: The Case of Pat Robertson's Supporters." *Journal of Politics* 50(1): 150-165. 1988.

Green, John C. and James L. Guth. "Controlling the Mischief of Faction: Party Support and Coalition Building Among Party Activists." In *Politics, Power and Professionalism*, ed. John C. Green. Rowman & Littlefield. Lanham, 1994.

Green, John C., James L. Guth and Kevin Hill. "Faith and Elections: The Christian Right in Congressional Campaigns 1978-1988." *Journal of Politics* 55(1): 80-91. 1993.

Green, John C., James L. Guth, and Clyde Wilcox. "Less than Conquerors: The Christian Right in State Republican Parties." In: Anne N. Costain and Andrew S. McFarland (eds.). *Social Movements and American Political Institutions.* Rowman & Littlefield. Lanham, 1998.

Green, John C., James L. Guth, Corwin Smidt, and Luman A. Kellstedt. *Religion and the Culture Wars: Dispatches from the Front.* Rowman & Littlefield. Lanham, 1996.

Green, John C., Mark J Rozell and Clyde Wilcox (ed.). *Prayers in the Precincts: The Christian Right in the 1998 Elections.* Georgetown University Press. Washington D.C., 2000.

Green, John C., Mark J. Rozell, and Clyde Wilcox (eds.). *The Christian Right in American Politics: Marching to the Millennium.* Georgetown University Press. Washington, D.C., 2003.

Green, John C., Mark J. Rozell, and Clyde Wilcox. "The Christian Right's Long Political March". In: Green, John C., Mark J. Rozell, and Clyde Wilcox (eds.). *The Christian Right in American Politics: Marching to the Millennium.* Georgetown University Press. Washington, D.C., 2003.

Green, John C., Mark J. Rozell, and Clyde Wilcox. "The Meaning of the March: A Direction for Future Research." In: Green, John C., Mark J. Rozell, and Clyde Wilcox (eds.). *The Christian Right in American Politics: Marching to the Millennium.* Georgetown University Press. Washington, D.C., 2003.

Greenberg, Anna. "The Church and the Revitalization of Politics and Community." *Political Science Quarterly*, Vol. 115. 2000.

Grimaldi, James. "Lobbyist Reed's 'Regret' Leaves Microsoft Officials Surprised." *The Washington Post*. April 13, 2000: A4.

Habermas, Juergen. "Neoconservative Cultural Criticism in the United States and West Germany." In: Habermas, Juergen. *The New Conservatism: Cultural Criticism and the Historians' Debate.* The MIT Press. Cambridge, 1989.

Hallow, Ralph Z. "Christian, But No Longer a Powerful Coalition." *The Washington Times.* March 14, 2001.

Hammond, Phillip E., Mark A. Shibley and Peter M. Solow. "Religion and Family Values in Presidential Voting". In: Bruce, Steve, Peter Kivisto and William H. Swatos, Jr. *The Rapture of Politics.* Transaction Publishers. London, 1995.

Harrell, David Edwin, Jr. *Pat Robertson: a Personal, Political and Religious Portrait.* Harper & Row. San Francisco, 1987.

Hershey, Majorie Randon. "The Campaign and the Media." In: Pomper, Gerald M. *The Election of 2000.* Seven Bridges Press. New York, 2001.

Hertzke, Allen D. *Representing God in Washington: The Role of Religious Lobbies in the American Polity.* Knoxville: University of Tennessee Press, 1988.

Hertzke, Allen. *Echoes of Discontent: Jesse Jackson, Pat Robertson, and the Resurgence of Populism.* CQ Press. Washington D.C., 1993.

Himmelfarb, Gertrude. "Religion in the 2000 Election." *Public Interest.* Spring 2001.

Hume, Ellen. "Pat Robertson Hopes to Turn Evangelical Fervor Into Political Constituency for a Presidential Bid." *Wall Street Journal.* July 16, 1986: 44.

Hunter, Allen. *Virtue with a Vengeance: The Pro-Family Politics of the New Right.* Ph.D. Dissertation, Brandeis University, 1985.

Independent Sector, The (Publ.). *From Belief to Commitment: The Activities and Finances Of Religious Congregations in the United States.* The Independent Sector. Washington, D.C., 1988.

Ireland, Patricia. "A Look At...Promise Keepers: Beware of 'Feel-Good Male Supremacy.'" *Washington Post.* September 7, 1997.

Isikoff, Michael. "The Money Machine." *Newsweek.* January24, 2000: 48.

Jorstad, Erling. *Popular Religion in America: The Evangelical Voice.* Greenwood Publishing Group. Westport,1993.

Jorstad, Erling. *The New Christian Right: 1981-1988.* Mellen Press. New York, 1988.

King, Wayne. "The Record of Pat Roberston On Religion and Government." *New York Times.* December 27, 1987: 1, 30.

Kintz, Linda and Julia Lesage (ed). *Media, Culture and the Religious Right.* University of Minnesota Press. Minneapolis, 1998.

Kintz, Linda. "Clarity, Mothers, and the Mass-Mediated National Soul: A Defense of Ambiguity." Kintz, Linda and Julia Lesage (ed). *Media, Culture and the Religious Right.* University of Minnesota Press. Minneapolis, 1998.

Kintz, Linda. "Culture and the Religious Right." In: Kintz, Linda and Julia Lesage (eds.). *Media, Culture and the Religious Right.* University of Minnesota Press. Minneapolis, 1998.

Kovach, Bill, and Tom Rosenstiel. "Campaign Lite." *Washington Monthly.* Jan. 2001.

Kristol, Irving. "The Political Dilemma of American Jews." *Commentary.* 78. July 1984. Page 25f.

LaHaye, Beverly. *The Spirit Controlled Woman.* Harvest House Publishers, Eugene, 1976.

Bibliography

LaHaye, Tim and Jerry B. Jenkins. *Left Behind: A Novel of the Earth's Last Days.* Tyndale House Publishers. Wheaton, 1995.

Goodstein, Laurie. "Focus on the GOP: Dobson fires a warning shot." *Minneapolis Star Tribune.* February 13, 1998: 16A.

Leege, David C. "Coalitions, Cues, Strategic Politics, and the Staying Power of the Religious Right." *Political Science and Politics.* 25:198-204. 1992.

Leege, David C. and Lyman A. Kellstedt. *Rediscovering the Religious Factor in American Politics.* M. E. Sharpe. New York, 1993.

Leggewie, Claus. *America first? Der Fall einer konservativen Revolution.* Fischer. Frankfurt am Main, 1997.

Lemke, Christiane. "Rechtsradikalismus in den USA – ein Vergleich." In: Perels, Joachim (Publ.). *Der Rechtsradikalismus – ein Randphänomen? Kritische Analysen.* Offizin-Verlag. Hannover, 2003.

Lesage, Julia. "Christian Coalition Leadership Training." In: Kintz, Linda and Julia Lesage (eds.). *Media, Culture and the Religious Right.* University of Minnesota Press. Minneapolis, 1998.

Lesage, Julia. "Christian Media." In: Kintz, Linda and Julia Lesage, (eds.). *Media, Culture and the Religious Right.* University of Minnesota Press. Minneapolis, 1998.

Levitt, Melissa and Katherine C. Naff. "Gender As a Political Constant: The More Things Change the More They Stay the Same." In: Wayne, Stephen J. and Clyde Wilcox (eds.). *The Election of the Century and What It Tells Us about the Future of American Politics.* M. E. Sharpe. London, 2002.

Lincoln and Mamiya. *The Black Church in the African American Experience.* Duke University Press. Durham, 1990.

Lipset, Seymour Martin. *American Exceptionalism: A Double Edged Sword.* W. W. Norton & Company. New York, 1997.

Loesche, Peter. "Thesen zum amerikanischen Konservatismus." In: *Aus Politik und Zeitgeschichte*, Volume 49. Dec 11, 1982: 37-45.

Lynn, Barry W. "Preacher Or President?: Politicians, Pandering And Campaign 2000." *Church & State.* Jan. 2000.

Maggleby, David B. (ed.). *Financing the 2000 Election.* Brookings Institution Press. Washington, D.C., 2002.

Maidens, Melinda (ed.). *Religion, Morality & the "New Right"*. Facts on File. New York, 1982.

Marsden, George M. *Understanding Fundamentalism and Evangelicalism*. William B. Erdmans. Grand Rapids, 1991.

Martin, William. *With God on Our Side: the Rise of the Religious Right in America*. Broadway Books. New York, 1997.

Martison, Oscar B. and E. A. Wilkening. "Religious Participation and Involvement in Local Politics throughout the Life Cycle." *Sociological Forces*. October 20, 1987: 309-18.

Marty, Martin E. *Religion in America since Mid-century*. Daedalus, 111. Winter 1982: pp 149 –163.

Mayer, Allan J. "A Tide of Born-Again Politics". *Newsweek*. September 15, 1980: 36.

McAdam, Doug and David S. Snow. *Social Movements: Readings on their Emergence, Mobilization and Dynamics*. Roxbury Publishing. Los Angeles, CA, 1997.

McCarthy, J. and Zald, M. "Resource Mobilization and Social Movements: A Partial Theory." *American Journal of Sociology*. 82, 1212-41. 1977.

McFarland, Elizabeth. "Lawyer 3rd in GOP." *The Arkansas Democrat Gazette*. February 6, 1992: B1.

Merton, Thomas and Paul M. Pearson (eds.). <u>Seeking Paradise: The Spirit of the Shakers</u>. Orbis Books. Chicago, 2003.

Milbrath, Lester and M. L. Goel. *Political Participation*. Rand McNally Publication Co. Chicago, 1977.

Minkenberg, Michael. "Die Christliche Rechte und die amerikanische Politik von der ersten bis zur zweiten Bush-Administration." In: *Aus Politik und Zeitgeschichte* Nr. 46. October 11, 2003.

Minkenberg, Michael. *Die neue radikale Rechte im Vergleich. USA, Frankreich, Deutschland*. Westdeutscher Verlag. Wiesbaden, 1998.

Minkenberg, Michael. *Neokonservatismus und Neue Rechte in den USA*. Nomos Verlag Gesellschaft. Baden Baden, 1990.

Moen, Matthew. *The Transformation of the Christian Right*. University of Alabama Press. Tuscaloosa, 1992.

Moen, Matthew. "From Revolution to Evolution: The Changing Nature of the Christian Right." In: Bruce, Steve, Peter Kivisto and William H. Swatos, Jr. *The Rapture of Politics*. Transaction Publishers. London, 1995.

Moen, Matthew. *The Religious Right and Congress*. Alabama University Press: Tuscaloosa, 1989.

Moreland, Laurence W., Robert P. Steed, and Todd A. Baker. "Ideology, Issues, and Realignment Among Southern Party Activists." In: Robert H. Swansbrough and David M. Brodsky (eds.). *The South's New Politics: Realignment and Dealignment*. University of South Carolina Press. Columbia, 1988.

Nash, Ronald H. *Evangelicals in America*. Abingdon Press. Nashville, 1987.

Oldfield, Duane. *The Right and the Righteous: The Christian Right Confronts the Republican Party*. Rowman & Littlefield. Lanham, MD, 1996.

Oropeza, B.J. *99 Reasons Why No One Knows When Christ Will Return*. Inter Varsity Press. Downers Grove, 1994.

Penning, James M. "Pat Robertson and the GOP: 1988 and Beyond." *Sociology of Religion* 55, no. 3. Fall 1994.

Penning, James M. "Pat Robertson and the GOP: 1988 and Beyond." In: Bruce, Steve, Peter Kivisto and William H. Swatos, Jr. *The Rapture of Politics*. Transaction Publishers. London, 1995.

Penning, James M. and Corwin E. Smidt. "Michigan 1998: The 'Right Stuff'." In: Green, John C., Mark J Rozell and Clyde Wilcox (eds.). *Prayers in the Precincts: The Christian Right in the 1998 Elections*. Georgetown University Press. Washington D.C., 2000.

Penning, James M., and Corwin Smidt. "What Coalition? Divisions in the Christian Right." *The Christian Century*. Jan. 15, 1997.

People for the American Way Homepage: http://www.pfaw.org/pfaw/general/default.aspx?oid=4307.

Perels, Joachim (Publ.). *Der Rechtsradikalismus – ein Randphänomen? Kritische Analysen*. Offizin-Verlag. Hannover, 2003.

Perels, Joachim. "Die Hannoversche Landeskirche im Nationalsozialismus 1935-45. Kritik eines Selbstbildes." *Beiheft Junge Kirche*. Hannover, September 1995: pp 1-23.

Peschek, Joseph G. *Policy Planning Organizations: Elite Agendas and America's Rightward Turn.* Temple University Press. Philadelphia, 1987.

Petchesky, Rosalind Pollack. *Abortion and Woman's Choice: The State, Sexuality and Reproductive Freedom.* Northeastern University Press. Boston, 1990.

Petchsky, Rosalind Pollack. "Antiabortion, Antifeminism, and the Rise of the New Right." *Feminist Studies.* Summer 1981.

Pfau, Michael. "The Subtle Nature of Presidential Debate Influence." *Argumentation and Advocacy.* 2002.

Phillips, Kevin. *Post-Conservative America.* Random House. New York, 1983.

Pines, Burton Y. "The U.S. and U.N.: Time for Reappraisal." In: P. Weyrich and C Marshner (eds.). *Future 21.* Devin-Adair. Greenwood, 1984: pp 70-89.

Plotz, David. http://slate.msn.com/id/1819.

Pomper, Gerald M. *The Election of 2000.* Seven Bridges Press. New York, 2001.

Prätorius, Rainer. *In God We Trust .* Beck. Muenchen, 2003.

Putnam, Robert. "Bowling Alone: America's Declining Social Capital." *Journal of Democracy.* January 6, 1995: 66.

Putnam, Robert. "Tuning In, Tuning Out: The Strange Disappearance of Social Capital in America." In: *PS: Political Science and Politics* 28. December 1995.

Ramsden, Graham P. "Media Coverage of Issues and Candidates: What Balance Is Appropriate in a Democracy?" *Political Science Quarterly.* 1996.

Reed, Ralph Eugene, Jr. *Fortress of Faith: Design and Experience at Southern Evangelical Colleges, 1830-1900.* Ph.D. Dissertation. Emory University, 1990.

Reed, Ralph Jr. "Introduction." In: *Contract with the American Family.* Moorings. Nashville, 1995: pp. ix-xiii.

Reed, Ralph Jr. "What Do Religious Conservatives Really Want? In: Michael Cromartie (ed.). *Disciples & Democracy.* Ethics and Public Policy Center. Washington, D.C., 1990: pp. 1-15.

Reed, Ralph. "Remarks to the Detroit Economic Club, January 17, 1995. Christian Coalition and an Agenda for the new Congress." In: *Contract with the American Family*. Moorings. Nashville, 1995: pp. 133-145.

Reed, Ralph. *Active Faith*. Free Press. New York, 1996.

Reed, Ralph. *Politically Incorrect*. Word Publishing. Dallas, 1994.

Rieger, Frank. *Der amerikanische Neokonservatismus*. Deutscher Universitaetsverlag. Wiesbaden, 1989.

Riesebrodt, Martin. "Der Protestantische Fundamentalismus in den USA, 1910-28." In: *Fundamentalismus als patriarchalische Protestbewegung. Amerikanische Protestanten (1910-28) und iranische Schiiten (1961-79) im Vergleich*. Tuebingen 1990.

Robertson, Pat and Bob Slosser. *The Secret Kingdom*. Thomas Nelson Publishers. Nashville, 1982.

Robertson, Pat. In: "Who's a Bigot?" *Washington Post*. February 24, 2000: p. A20.

Robertson, Pat. Quoted in: "Preachers in Politics." *US News & World Report*. September 24, 1979.

Robertson, Pat. Quoted in: "Evangelicals 'Reinforce Mainstream America'" interview. *U.S. News & World Report*. November 4, 1985: 75.

Robertson, Pat. *America's Dates with Destiny*. Thomas Nelson. Nashville, 1986.

Robertson, Pat. *Answers to 200 Life's Most Probing Questions*. Thomas Nelson Publisher. Nashville, 1984.

Robertson, Pat. Quoted in "With Little Time to Exult or Weep, Candidates Get Set for the Next Round." *New York Times*. February 10, 1988: I22.

Robertson, Pat. Remarks on *The 700 Club*. Christian Broadcasting Network. January 11, 1985.

Robertson, Pat. *The End of the Age*. Word Publishing. Dallas, 1995.

Robertson, Pat. *The New Millennium*. Word Publishing. Dallas, 1990.

Robertson, Pat. *The New World Order*. Word Publishing. Dallas, 1991.

Robertson, Pat. *The Plan*. Thomas Nelson Publisher. Nashville, 1998.

Robertson, Pat. *The Secret Kingdom: Your Path to Peace, Love and Financial Security*. 2nd Edition. Word Publishing. Dallas, 1992.

Robertson, Pat. *The Turning Tide*. Word Publishing. Dallas, 1993.

Rozell, Mark and Clyde Wilcox. *Second Coming*. John Hopkins University Press. Washington, D.C., 1996.

Rozell, Mark and Clyde Wilcox. *God at the Grassroots: The Christian Right in the 1996 Elections*. Rowman & Littlefield. Lanham, MD, 1997.

Rozell, Mark and Clyde Wilcox. *Interest Groups in American Campaigns*. Congressional Quarterly Press. Washington D.C., 1999.

Rozell, Mark J. and Clyde Wilcox. *God at the Grassroots: The Christian Right in the 1994 Elections*. Rowman & Littlefield. Lanham, MD, 1995.

Rozell, Mark J. "...Or Influential as Ever?" *The Washington Post*. March 1, 2000: pp. A17.

Rozell, Mark. "Piety, Politics, and Pluralism: Religion, the Courts, and the 2000 Elections." In: Mary Segers (ed.). *Religion and Liberal Democracy: Piety, Politics and Pluralism*. Rowman & Littlefield Pub. Lanham, 2002.

Sawyer Allen, Martha. "Evangelical Christianity Comes of Age." *Minneapolis Star Tribune*. March 2, 2003: pp. 01A.

Schaefer, Brett D. *The International Criminal Court: Threatening U.S. Sovereignty and Security*. Executive Memorandum. The Heritage Foundation. Volume No. 537. July 2, 1998.

Schissler, Jakob (ed.). *Neokonservatismus in den USA*. Westdeutscher Verlag. Opladen, 1983.

Schulze, Laurie and Frances Guilfoyle. "Facts Don't Hate; They Just Are." In: Kintz, Linda and Julia Lesage (eds.). *Media, Culture and the Religious Right*. University of Minnesota Press. Minneapolis, 1998.

Scofield, Cyrus I. *The Scofield Reference Bible*. Oxford University Press. Oxford, 1909.

Sedgwick, John. "The GOP's Three Amigos." *Newsweek*. January 9, 1995: pp. 38-40.

Shribman, David. "Going Mainstream: Religious Right Drops High-Profile Tactics, Works on Local Level." *Wall Street Journal*. September 26, 1989: A1.

Silk, Mark (ed.). *Religion and American Politics: The 2000 Election in Context.* Center for the Study of Religion in Public Life. Hartford, 2000.

Simec, Lisa. *Christian Coalition facing two lawsuits being brought by current and former employees claiming racial segregation and discrimination.* Publication: Weekend Edition – National Public Radio. March 31, 2001.

Smith, Christian. *Christian America? What Evangelicals Really Want.* University of California Press. Berkley, 2000.

Soper, Christopher. J. *Ideology, Political Institutions, and Social Movement Activism: A Comparison of the Mobilization of British and American Evangelicals.* PhD. Dissertation. Yale University 1992.

Spring, Baker. *Missile Defense Programs Lag Behind the Threat.* In: http://www.heritage.org/views/2002/ed041802.html.

Steinfels, Peter. *The Neoconservatives.* Simon and Schuster. New York, 1979.

Stern, Fritz. *The Politics of Cultural Despair.* University of California Press. Berkely, 1961.

Stodghill et al.: "God of Our Fathers: The Promise Keepers are Bringing Their Manly Crusade to Washington. Are The Men Behaving Nobly? Or a Threat to Freedom?" *Time Magazine.* October 6, 1997.

Swomley, John M. "Storm Troopers in the Culture War." In: *The Humanist.* September/October 1997.

Tarrow, Sidney. "The Very Excess of Democracy: State Building and Contentious Politics in America." In: Anne Costain and Andrew McFarland (eds.). *Social Movements and American Political Institutions.* Rowman & Littlefield. Lanham, MD, 1995.

Tarrow, Sidney. *Power in Movement.* Cambridge University Press. Cambridge, 1998.

Tipton, Steven M. *Getting Saved from the Sixties.* University of California Press. Berkeley, 1982.

Tocqueville, Alexis de. *Ueber die Demokratie in Amerika, 2. Teil, Werke und Briefe.* Jacob P. Mayer (ed). Reclam. Ditzingen, 1985.

Turner, R. H. and L. M. Killian. *Collective Behavior.* Prentice-Hall. Englewood Cliffs, NJ, 1965.

Utter, Glenn H. and John W. Storey. *The Religious Right: A Reference Handbook*. ABC-Clio. Santa Barbara, 1995.

Van Natta, Don Jr. "Bush Uses Family Ties to Build Up Treasury." *New York Times*. January 30, 2000b: A12.

Van Natta, Don Jr. "Early Contributions Opened the Floodgates for Bush." *New York Times*. January 20, 2000a: A20.

Verba, Sidney, Kay Lehman Schlozman, and Henry E. Brady. *Voice and Equality: Civic Voluntarism in American Politics*. Harvard University Press. Cambridge, 1995.

Viguerie, Richard. *The New Right: We're Ready to Lead*. The Viguerie Co. Falls Church, 1980.

Wald, Kenneth. *Religion and Politics in the United States*. St. Martin's Press. New York, 1987.

Warner, R. S. *New Wine in Old Wineskins*. University of California Press. Berkeley, 1988.

Watson, Justin. *The Christian Coalition: Dreams of Restoration, Demands for Recognition*. St. Martin's Griffin. New York, 1997.

Wayne, Stephen J. and Clyde Wilcox (eds.). *The Election of the Century and What It Tells Us About the Future of American Politics*. M. E. Sharpe. London, 2002.

Wertkin, Jeffrey A. "Election2000.com: Internet Use and the American Voter." In: Wayne, Stephen J. and Clyde Wilcox (eds.). *The Election of the Century and What It Tells Us about the Future of American Politics*. M. E. Sharpe. London, 2002.

Weyrich, Paul. "The Cultural Right's Hot New Agenda." *Washington Post*. May 4, 1986: p. C4f.

Weyrich, Paul. "The Reform of the Democratic Institutions: The National Initiative." In: P. Weyrich and C. Marshner (eds.). *Future 21*. Devin-Adair. Greenwich, 1984: pp. 222-229.

Wilcox, Clyde and Mark J. Rozell. "Conclusion: The Christian Right in Campaign '98." In: Green, John C., Mark J. Rozell and Clyde Wilcox (eds.). *Prayers in the Precincts: The Christian Right in the 1998 Elections*. Georgetown University Press. Washington D.C., 2000.

Wilcox, Clyde. *Onward Christian Soldiers? The Religious Right in American Politics*. 2nd Edition. Westview Press. Colorado, 2000.

Wilcox, Clyde. "Premillennialists at the Millennium: Some Reflections on the Christian Right in the Twenty-first Century." In: Bruce, Steve, Peter Kivisto and William H. Swatos, Jr. *The Rapture of Politics.* Transaction Publishers. London, 1995.

Wilcox, Clyde. "Wither the Christian Right? The Elections and Beyond." In: Wayne, Stephen J. and Clyde Wilcox (eds.). *The Election of the Century and What It Tells Us about the Future of American Politics.* M. E. Sharpe. London, 2002.

Williams Mike. "Election '98 Gubernatorial Races; Florida; Bush is leaving no base untouched." *The Atlanta Journal Constitution.* October 18, 1998: G5.

Williams, Anna. "Conservative Media Activism: The Free Congress Foundation and National Empowerment Television." In: Kintz, Linda and Julia Lesage (eds.). *Media, Culture and the Religious Right.* University of Minnesota Press. Minneapolis, 1998.

Wuthnow, Robert. *Mobilizing Civic Engagement: The Changing Impact of Religious Involvement.* Department of Sociology, Princeton University. 1997: p. 14.

Zald, Mayer N. and John D. McCarthy. *Social Movements in an Organizational Society.* Transaction Publications. New Brunswick, NJ, 1987.

Appendix

6. Appendix

Speeches

George W. Bush
Videotaped Remarks to the Christian Coalition Road to Victory Luncheon
September 30, 2000

Differences in Issue Positions between Gore and Myself

The road ahead is a lot shorter since I joined you at last year's convention. These are the final days of the campaign - and the final days of the Clinton-Gore era. You and I know there's a lot at stake in this election. Everywhere I go, I see our message taking hold - a message of change, reform, and integrity. Americans are not asking for bigger, more intrusive government. But they deserve a government that respects their values, and gives them the tools to dream and build and succeed on their own. On taxes, here is my plan: If you pay income taxes, you get tax relief. If you are a low or moderate income worker, you get the biggest percentage tax cut of all.

We're going to cut the marriage penalty, and get rid of the death tax. And I believe, as a matter of principle that no one in America should pay more than a third of his or her income to the federal government. My opponent's theory is that only the "right" people should get tax relief. That's what Al Gore called them at his convention, the "right" people. But there are no right Americans or wrong Americans. Tax relief should be aimed at one big target, so you can't miss: they should be aimed at all Americans who pay income taxes.

On the budget, I've offered a detailed plan that includes tax relief, and leaves three of every four dollars of the surplus for urgent priorities: Social Security, Medicare, and prescription drugs, debt reduction, education, health and rebuilding our military so that we can keep the peace.

My opponent has a plan for the non-Social Security surplus: He would spend it on new programs. He would spend it all - and then some. After a long career in Washington, my opponent is convinced the surplus is the government's money. But you and I know differently, we know the surplus is the people's money.

On education, I have a plan to ensure that every school has high standards, every parent has real options, and no child is left behind. We are going to restore discipline and safety - giving authority to the teacher in the classroom and the principal down the hall.

The Vice President talks about "the people versus the powerful." But in all his plans, who ends up with the power? Who always ends up making the choices? Not the taxpayers, but the tax collectors. Not parents, or even teachers, but some distant central office. He says he wants to help "the people." If only he would trust them.

He is trying to have it both ways. But, as Ronald Reagan said, "You can't be for big government, big bureaucracy, and still be for the little guy." Like Ronald Reagan, I believe that the freedom we cherish ultimately depends on the values our families teach. We must give our children a spirit of moral courage, because their character is our destiny.

We must tell them, with clarity and confidence, that drugs and alcohol can destroy you, and bigotry disfigures the heart. Our schools must support the ideals of parents, elevating character and abstinence from afterthoughts to urgent goals.

We must help protect our children, in our schools and streets, by finally and strictly enforcing our nation's gun laws. And we must teach our children the values that defeat violence.

Should I be elected, I will lead our nation toward a culture that values life - the life of the elderly and the sick, the life of the young, and the life of the unborn.
I know good people disagree on this issue, but surely we can agree on ways to value life by promoting adoption and parental notification. And when Congress sends me a bill against partial-birth abortion, I will sign it into law.

Freedom, responsibility, family - this is my message, and before the campaign is over, I will carry it as far and wide as I can. And I need your help. This may be the closest election in 40 years. That means every day will count. Every vote will count. Everything we do will make a difference.

If we work together, we are on the road to victory.

We will give America afresh start after a season of cynicism. And next January, should I be fortunate to become the President, when I put my hand on the Bible, I will swear to not only uphold the laws of our land, I will swear to uphold the honor and dignity of the office to which I have been elected, so help me God.

Appendix

Welfare Reform and Child Care
George W. Bush

Republican National Convention 2000
Philadelphia, Pennsylvania

Party Platform: A New Prosperity: Seats for All at the Welcome Table

"America has been successful because it offers a realistic shot at a better life. America has been successful because poverty has been a stage, not a fate. America has been successful because anyone can ascend the ladder and transcend their birth." — George W. Bush

We want to expand opportunity instead of government. Governor Bush calls this "the Duty of Hope." We see it as our duty to act. But whatever we name it, the goal is the same — to give hope and real upward mobility to those who have never known either. It's clear that the old left-liberal order of social policy has collapsed in failure; and its failure was the most egregious among whom it most professed to serve: the poor and those on the margins of society.

The time is here to act, to bring hope, to expand opportunity. Republican governors throughout the country sparked a revolution that brought about the greatest social policy change in nearly 60 years — welfare reform. Inspired by the innovative reforms of Republican governors that successfully moved families from welfare dependence to the independence of work, congressional Republicans passed landmark welfare reform legislation in 1996 that has helped millions of Americans break the cycle of welfare and gain independence for their families. Because of that legislation — turning welfare resources and decision- making back to the states, with the understanding that recipients must meet a work requirement and such assistance would be only temporary — about six million Americans are now gainfully employed, many for the first time. We salute them.

And now it's time to take more steps in the right direction by helping these families climb the opportunity ladder. It won't be easy, but welfare reform wasn't easy either, though the results were surely worth the fight.

Here are our next steps:

Reward work with tax reform that takes 6 million families off the tax rolls, cuts the rate for those who remain on the rolls, and doubles the child tax credit to $1,000. Implement the "American Dream Down Payment" program, which will allow a half million families who currently draw federal rental assistance to become homeowners, and allow families receiving federal rental payments to apply one year's worth of their existing assistance money toward the purchase of their own first home, thus becoming independent of any further government housing assistance. This approach builds upon our long standing commitment to resident management of public housing and other initiatives. Increase the supply of affordable housing for low-income working families and rehabilitate abandoned housing that blights neighborhoods by establishing the Renewing the Dream tax credit. This investor-based tax credit will create or renovate more than 100,000 single-family housing units in distressed communities. Build savings and personal wealth through Individual Development Accounts, in partnership with banks, to accelerate the savings of low income earners. For many individuals, poverty signals more than the lack of money.

It often represents obstacles that cannot be overcome with just a paycheck. These are the challenging cases, where government aid is least effective. These, too, are the situations where neighborhood and faithbased intervention has its greatest power. For this reason, the Republican Congress mandated charitable choice in the welfare reform law of 1996, allowing states to contract with faith-based providers for welfare services on the same basis as any other providers. The current administration has done its utmost to block the implementation of that provision, insisting that all symbols of religion must be removed or covered over — precisely what the 1996 provisions set out to prevent. The result is that many of the most successful service programs are essentially blacklisted because they will neither conceal nor compromise the faith that makes them so effective in changing lives. While this is unfair to faith-based organizations, it is unjust to those whom they could help conquer abuse, addiction, and hopelessness.

Texas was the first state to implement charitable choice in welfare, and its governor intends to expand it to all federally-funded human services programs. We support his plans to unbar the gates of the government ghetto, inviting into the American dream those who are now in its shadows and using the dedication and expertise of faith communities to make it happen.

This is what we propose: Apply charitable Choice to all federal social service programs. Encourage an outpouring of giving by extending the current federal charity tax deduction to the 70 percent of all tax filers who do

Appendix

not itemize their deductions and by allowing people to make donations tax-free from their IRAs.

Promote corporate giving by raising the cap on their charitable deductions and assuring them liability protection for their in-kind donations.

The renewal of entire communities is an awesome task and involves one human face, one human heart at a time. But the American people have a long and seasoned history of working wonders. Government does have a role to play, but as a partner, not a rival, to the armies of compassion. These forces have roots in the areas they serve, and their leaders are people to whom the disadvantaged are not statistics, but neighbors, friends, and moral individuals created in the image of God. With these approaches government becomes a partner with community and faith-based providers in supporting families and children and helping them improve their opportunities for a better life.

Inaugural Speech George W. Bush, January 20, 2001.

This peaceful transfer of authority is rare in history, yet common in our country. With a simple oath, we affirm old traditions, and make new beginnings. As I begin, I thank President Clinton for his service to our nation. And I thank Vice President Gore for a contest conducted with spirit, and ended with grace.

I am honored and humbled to stand here, where so many of America's leaders have come before me, and so many will follow.

We have a place, all of us, in a long story; a story we continue, but whose end we will not see. It is the story of a new world that became a friend and liberator of the old. The story of a slave-holding society that became a servant of freedom. The story of a power that went into world to protect but not possess, to defend but not to conquer. It is the American story; a story of flawed and fallible people, united across the generations by grand and enduring ideals.

The grandest of these ideals is an unfolding American promise: that everyone belongs, that everyone deserves a chance, that no insignificant person was ever born. Americans are called to enact this promise in our lives and in our laws. And though our nation has sometimes halted, and sometimes delayed, we must follow no other course.

Through much of the last century, America's faith in freedom and democracy was a rock in a raging sea. Now it is a seed upon the wind, taking root in many nations. Our democratic faith is more than the creed of our country, it is the inborn hope of our humanity; an ideal we carry but do not own, a trust we bear and pass along. And even after nearly 225 years, we have a long way yet to travel.

While many of our citizens prosper, others doubt the promise - even the justice - of our own country. The ambitions of some Americans are limited by failing schools, and hidden prejudice, and the circumstances of their birth. And sometimes our differences run so deep, it seems we share a continent, but not a country.

We do not accept this, and will not allow it. Our unity, our union, is the serious work of leaders and citizens in every generation. And this is my solemn pledge: I will work to build a single nation of justice and opportunity.

Appendix

I know this is within our reach, because we are guided by a power larger than ourselves, Who creates us equal in His image.

And we are confident in principles that unite and lead us onward.

America has never been united by blood or birth or soil. We are bound by ideals that move us beyond our backgrounds, lift us above our interests, and teach us what it means to be citizens. Every child must be taught these principles. Every citizen must uphold them. And every immigrant, by embracing these ideals, makes our country more, not less, American.

Today we affirm a new commitment to live out our nation's promise through civility, courage, compassion and character. America, at its best, matches a commitment to principle with a concern for civility. A civil society demands from each of us good will and respect, fair dealing and forgiveness.

Some seem to believe that our politics can afford to be petty because, in a time of peace, the stakes of our debates appear small. But the stakes, for America, are never small. If our country does not lead the cause of freedom, it will not be led. If we do not turn the hearts of children toward knowledge and character, we will lose their gifts and undermine their idealism. If we permit our economy to drift and decline, the vulnerable will suffer most.

We must live up to the calling we share. Civility is not a tactic or a sentiment. It is the determined choice of trust over cynicism, of community over chaos. And this commitment, if we keep it, is a way to shared accomplishment.

America, at its best, is also courageous.

Our national courage has been clear in times of depression and war, when defeating common dangers defined our common good. Now we must choose if the example of our fathers and mothers will inspire us or condemn us. We must show courage in a time of blessing, by confronting problems instead of passing them on to future generations.

Together we will reclaim America's schools, before ignorance and apathy claim more young lives. We will reform Social Security and Medicare, sparing our children from struggles we have the power to prevent. We will reduce taxes, to recover the momentum of our economy and reward the effort and enterprise of working Americans. We will build our defenses beyond challenge, lest weakness invite challenge. We will confront weapons of mass destruction, so that a new century is spared new horrors.

The enemies of liberty and our country should make no mistake. America remains engaged in the world, by history and by choice, shaping a balance of power that favors freedom. We will defend our allies and our interests. We will show purpose without arrogance. We will meet aggression and bad faith with resolve and strength. And to all nations, we will speak for the values that gave our nation birth.

America, at its best, is compassionate.

In the quiet of American conscience, we know that deep, persistent poverty is unworthy of our nation's promise. And whatever our views of its cause, we can agree that children at risk are not at fault. Abandonment and abuse are not acts of God, they are failures of love. And the proliferation of prisons, however necessary, is no substitute for hope and order in our souls.

Where there is suffering, there is duty. Americans in need are not strangers, they are citizens; not problems, but priorities; and all of us are diminished when any are hopeless.

Government has great responsibilities, for public safety and public health, for civil rights and common schools. Yet compassion is the work of a nation, not just a government. And some needs and hurts are so deep they will only respond to a mentor's touch or a pastor's prayer. Church and charity, synagogue and mosque, lend our communities their humanity, and they will have an honored place in our plans and laws.
Many in our country do not know the pain of poverty. But we can listen to those who do. And I can pledge our nation to a goal: When we see that wounded traveler on the road to Jericho, we will not pass to the other side.

America, at its best, is a place where personal responsibility is valued and expected.

Encouraging responsibility is not a search for scapegoats, it is a call to conscience. And though it requires sacrifice, it brings a deeper fulfillment. We find the fullness of life, not only in options, but in commitments. And we find that children and community are the commitments that set us free.

Our public interest depends on private character; on civic duty and family bonds and basic fairness; on uncounted, unhonored acts of decency which give direction to our freedom.

Appendix

Sometimes in life we are called to do great things. But as a saint of our times has said, every day we are called to do small things with great love. The most important tasks of a democracy are done by everyone.

I will live and lead by these principles: to advance my convictions with civility; to pursue the public interest with courage; to speak for greater justice and compassion; to call for responsibility, and try to live it as well. In all these ways, I will bring the values of our history to the care of our times.

What you do is as important as anything government does. I ask you to seek a common good beyond your comfort; to defend needed reforms against easy attacks; to serve your nation, beginning with your neighbor. I ask you to be citizens. Citizens, not spectators. Citizens, not subjects. Responsible citizens, building communities of service and a nation of character.

Americans are generous and strong and decent, not because we believe in ourselves, but because we hold beliefs beyond ourselves. When this spirit of citizenship is missing, no government program can replace it. When this spirit is present, no wrong can stand against it.

After the Declaration of Independence was signed, Virginia statesman John Page wrote to Thomas Jefferson: "We know the Race is not to the swift nor the Battle to the Strong. Do you not think an Angel rides in the Whirlwind and directs this Storm?"

Much time has passed since Jefferson arrived for his inaugural. The years and changes accumulate. But the themes of this day he would know: our nation's grand story of courage, and its simple dream of dignity.

We are not this story's Author, Who fills time and eternity with His purpose. Yet His purpose is achieved in our duty; and duty is fulfilled in service to one another.

Never tiring, never yielding, never finishing, we renew that purpose today: to make our country more just and generous; to affirm the dignity of our lives and every life.

This work continues. This story goes on. And an angel still rides in the whirlwind and directs this storm.

God bless you, and God bless our country.

Wissenschaftliche Paperbacks
Politikwissenschaft

Hartmut Elsenhans
Das Internationale System zwischen Zivilgesellschaft und Rente
Gegen derzeitige Theorieangebote für die Erklärung der Ursachen und die Auswirkungen wachsender transnationaler und internationaler Verflechtung setzt das hier vorliegende Konzept eine stark durch politökonomische Überlegungen integrierte Perspektive, die auf politologischen, soziologischen, ökonomischen und philosophischen Ansatzpunkten aufbaut. Mit diesem Konzept soll gezeigt werden, daß der durch Produktionsauslagerungen/ Direktinvestitionen/ neue Muster der internationalen Arbeitsteilung gekennzeichnete (im weiteren als Transnationalisierung von Wirtschaftsbeziehungen bezeichnete) kapitalistische Impuls zur Integration der bisher nicht in die Weltwirtschaft voll integrierten Peripherie weiterhin zu schwach ist, als daß dort nichtmarktwirtschaftliche Formen der Aneignung von Überschuß entscheidend zurückgedrängt werden können. Das sich herausbildende internationale System ist deshalb durch miteinander verschränkte Strukturen von Markt- und Nichtmarktökonomie gekennzeichnet, die nur unter bestimmten Voraussetzungen synergetische Effekte in Richtung einer autonomen und zivilisierten Weltzivilgesellschaft entfalten werden. Dabei treten neue Strukturen von Nichtmarktökonomie auf transnationaler Ebene auf, während der Wiederaufstieg von Renten die zivilgesellschaftlichen Grundlagen funktionierender oder potentiell zu Funktionsfähigkeit zu bringender, dann kapitalistischer Systeme auf internationaler und lokaler Ebene eher behindert.
Bd. 6, 2001, 140 S., 12,90 €, br.,
ISBN 3-8258-4837-x

Klaus Schubert
Innovation und Ordnung
In einer evolutionär voranschreitenden Welt sind statische Politikmodelle und -theorien problematisch. Deshalb lohnt es sich, die wichtigste Quelle für die Entstehung der policy-analysis, den Pragmatismus, als dynamische, demokratieendogene politisch-philosophische Strömung zu rekonstruieren. Dies geschieht im ersten Teil der Studie. Der zweite Teil trägt zum Verständnis des daraus folgenden politikwissenschaftlichen Ansatzes bei. Darüber hinaus wird durch eine konstruktiv-spekulative Argumentation versucht, die z. Z. wenig innovative Theorie- und Methodendiskussion in der Politikwissenschaft anzuregen.
Bd. 7, 2003, 224 S., 25,90 €, br.,
ISBN 3-8258-6091-4

Politik: Forschung und Wissenschaft

Klaus Segbers; Kerstin Imbusch (eds.)
The Globalization of Eastern Europe
Teaching International Relations Without Borders
Bd. 1, 2000, 600 S., 35,90 €, br.,
ISBN 3-8258-4729-2

Hartwig Hummel; Ulrich Menzel (Hg.)
Die Ethnisierung internationaler Wirtschaftsbeziehungen und daraus resultierende Konflikte
Mit Beiträgen von Annabelle Gambe, Hartwig Hummel, Ulrich Menzel und Birgit Wehrhöfer
Bd. 2, 2001, 272 S., 30,90 €, br.,
ISBN 3-8258-4836-1

Theodor Ebert
Opponieren und Regieren mit gewaltfreien Mitteln
Pazifismus – Grundsätze und Erfahrungen für das 21. Jahrhundert. Band 1
Bd. 3, 2001, 328 S., 20,90 €, br.,
ISBN 3-8258-5706-9

L**IT** Verlag Münster – Berlin – Hamburg – London – Wien
Grevener Str./Fresnostr. 2 48159 Münster
Tel.: 0251 – 62 032 22 – Fax: 0251 – 23 19 72
e-Mail: vertrieb@lit-verlag.de – http://www.lit-verlag.de

Theodor Ebert
Der Kosovo-Krieg aus pazifistischer Sicht
Pazifismus – Grundsätze und Erfahrungen für das 21. Jahrhundert. Band 2
Mit dem Luftkrieg der NATO gegen Jugoslawien begann für den deutschen Nachkriegspazifismus ein neues Zeitalter. Ebert hat sich über Jahrzehnte als Konfliktforscher und Schriftleiter der Zeitschrift "Gewaltfreie Aktion" mit den Möglichkeiten gewaltfreier Konfliktbearbeitung befasst. Von ihm stammt der erste Entwurf für einen Zivilen Friedensdienst als Alternative zum Militär. Aus dem Vorwort: "Wer sich einbildet, auch in Zukunft ließe sich aus großer Höhe mit Bomben politischer Gehorsam erzwingen, unterschätzt die Möglichkeiten, die fanatische Terroristen haben, in fahrlässiger Weise. Jedes Atomkraftwerk ist eine stationäre Atombombe, die von Terroristen mit geringem Aufwand in ein Tschernobyl verwandelt werden kann. Wir haben allen Grund, schleunigst über zivile Alternativen zu militärischen Einsätzen nachzudenken und die vorhandene Ansätze solch ziviler Alternativen zu entwickeln."
Bd. 4, 2001, 176 S., 12,90 €, br.,
ISBN 3-8258-5707-7

Wolfgang Gieler
Handbuch der Ausländer- und Zuwanderungspolitik
Von Afghanistan bis Zypern
In der Literatur zur Ausländer- und Zuwanderungspolitik fehlt ein Handbuch, dass einen schnellen und kompakten Überblick dieses Politikbereichs ermöglicht. Das vorliegende Handbuch bemüht sich diese wissenschaftliche Lücke zu schließen. Thematisiert werden die Ausländer- und Zuwanderungspolitik weltweiter Staaten von Afghanistan bis Zypern. Zentrale Fragestellung ist dabei der Umgang mit Fremden, das heißt mit Nicht-Inländern im jeweiligen Staat. Hierbei werden insbesondere politische, soziale, rechtliche, wirtschaftliche und kulturelle Aspekte mitberücksichtigt. Um eine Kompatibilität der Beiträge herzustellen beinhaltet jeder Beitrag darüber hinaus eine Zusammenstellung der historischen Grunddaten und eine Tabelle zur jeweiligen Anzahl der im Staat lebenden Ausländer. Die vorgelegte Publikation versteht sich als ein grundlegendes Nachschlagewerk. Neben dem universitären Bereich richtet es sich besonders an die gesellschaftspolitisch interessierte Öffentlichkeit und den auf sozialwissenschaftlichen Kenntnissen angewiesenen Personen in Politik, Verwaltung, Medien, Bildungseinrichtungen und Migranten-Organisationen.
Bd. 6, 2003, 768 S., 98,90 €, gb.,
ISBN 3-8258-6444-8

Harald Barrios; Martin Beck; Andreas Boeckh; Klaus Segbers (Eds)
Resistance to Globalization
Political Struggle and Cultural Resilience in the Middle East, Russia, and Latin America
This volume is an important contribution to the empirical research on what globalization means in different world regions. "Resistance" here has a double meaning: It can signify active, intentional resistance to tendencies which are rejected on political or moral grounds by presenting alternative discourses and concepts founded in specific cultural and national traditions. It can also mean resilience with regard to globalization pressures in the sense that traditional patterns of development and politics are resistant to change. The book shows the that the local, sub-national, national, and regional patterns of politics and development coexist with globalized structures without yielding very much ground and in ways which may turn out to be a serious barrier to further globalization. Case studies presented focus on Venezuela, Brazil, the Middle East, Iran, and Russia.
Bd. 7, 2003, 184 S., 20,90 €, br.,
ISBN 3-8258-6749-8

LIT Verlag Münster – Berlin – Hamburg – London – Wien
Grevener Str./Fresnostr. 2 48159 Münster
Tel.: 0251 – 62 032 22 – Fax: 0251 – 23 19 72
E-Mail: vertrieb@lit-verlag.de – http://www.lit-verlag.de

Michael Neu; Wolfgang Gieler; Jürgen Bellers (Hg.)
Handbuch der Außenwirtschaftspolitiken: Staaten und Organisationen
Afrika, Amerika, Asien, Europa, Ozeanien
Das vorliegende Handbuch ist die erste umfassende Darstellung der Außenwirtschaftspolitiken der Staaten dieser Welt. Die klar strukturierten Beiträge sind in verständlicher Sprache verfasst. Sie geben Wissenschaftlern, Studierenden und sonstigen interessierten Personen des öffentlichen und privaten Lebens einen fundierten und soliden Überblick über die nationalen Wirtschaftsstrukturen und Außenwirtschaftsbeziehungen der einzelnen Länder. Darüber hinaus werden in diesem Zusammenhang relevante internationale Organisationen behandelt.
Bd. 8 (2 Bde.), 2004, 1136 S., 149,90 €, br., ISBN 3-8258-6920-2

Ellen Bos; Antje Helmerich
Neue Bedrohung Terrorismus
Der 11. September 2001 und die Folgen.
Unter Mitarbeit von Barry Adams und Harald Wilkoszewski
Die terroristischen Anschläge des 11. September 2001 haben die Weltöffentlichkeit erschüttert. Ihre weitreichenden Auswirkungen auf die Lebenswirklichkeit des Einzelnen, den Handlungsspielraum der Nationalstaaten und das internationale System stehen im Mittelpunkt des Sammelbandes. Er basiert auf einer Ringvorlesung, in der sich Wissenschaftler der Ludwig-Maximilians-Universität München aus den Fächern Amerikanistik, Jura, Geschichte, Politik-, Religions-, Kommunikations- und Wirtschaftswissenschaft mit den geistigen Hintergründen und den Konsequenzen des Terrorismus auseinandersetzten.
Bd. 9, 2003, 232 S., 19,90 €, br., ISBN 3-8258-7099-5

Heinz-Gerhard Justenhoven; James Turner (Eds.)
Rethinking the State in the Age of Globalisation
Catholic Thought and Contemporary Political Theory
Since Jean Bodin and Thomas Hobbes, political theorists have depicted the state as "sovereign" because it holds preeminent authority over all the denizens belonging to its geographically defined territory. From the Peace of Westphalia in 1648 until the beginning of World War I in 1914, the essential responsiblities ascribcd to the sovereign state were maintaining internal and external security and promoting domestic prosperity. This idea of "the state" in political theory is clearly inadequate to the realities of national governments and international relations at the beginning of the twenty-first century. During the twentieth century, the sovereign state, as a reality and an idea, has been variously challenged from without and within its borders. Where will the state head in the age of globalisation? Can Catholic polilical thinking contribute to an adequate concept of statehood and government? A group of German and American scholars were asked to explore specific ways in which the intellectual traditions of Catholicism might help our effort lo rethink the state. The debate is guided by the conviction that these intellectual resources will prove valuable to political theorists as they work to revise our understanding of the state.
Bd. 10, 2003, 240 S., 19,90 €, br., ISBN 3-8258-7249-1

Gesine Foljanty-Jost (ed.)
Japan in the 1990s
Crisis as an impetus for change
The 1990s in Japan have been a period of far-reaching changes in Japanese society, which have not come to an end yet. These developments demand a reexamination of our accumulated knowledge of Japan. This volume looks at them from different perspectives; the contributions deal with issues from the fields of economy, education, political and social science. The volume is a collection of

papers from the 2002 meeting of the German Association of Social Scientific Research of Japan (VSJF) at Halle-Wittenberg University.
Bd. 11, 2004, 224 S., 24,90 €, br.,
ISBN 3-8258-7346-3

Wolfgang Gieler; Dietmar Fricke (Hg.)
Handbuch Europäischer Migrationspolitiken
Die EU-Länder und die Beitrittskandidaten
Migrationspolitik ist ein zentrales Thema in der politischen Diskussion. Es ist zu erwarten, dass sowohl die Diskussion um eine restriktivere Migrationspolitik als auch die sich dort abbildenden Befürchtungen und Stereotype in der Bevölkerung mit der EU-Osterweiterung neue Nahrung erhalten. Andererseits ist das allgemeine Wissen über die jeweilige Migrationspolitik der EU insgesamt und noch mehr die der einzelnen EU-Länder als auch die der Beitrittskandidaten sehr gering. Das vorliegende Handbuch möchte hier ein Lücke schließen und zur Versachlichung der Diskussion beitragen. Die Publikation versteht sich als ein grundlegendes Nachschlagewerk, das eine schnelle und differenzierte Orientierungshilfe in dem komplexen Feld der europäischen Migrationspolitiken ermöglichen soll.
Bd. 12, 2004, 320 S., 29,90 €, gb.,
ISBN 3-8258-7509-1

Patrick van Schie; Gerrit Voerman (Hg.)
The dividing line between success and failure
A comparison of liberalism in the Netherlands and Germany in the 19th and 20th centuries
Since the Second World War, liberalism has been much stronger in the Netherlands than in Germany. The present volume compares the development of liberalism in both countries – which took place under quite different conditions and without much mutual interaction – from the early beginnings in the nineteenth century down to the twenty-first century. It tries to explain why Dutch liberals are nowadays doing better than their German counterparts. Patrick van Schie is director of the Telders Foundation, the Dutch liberal think thank. Gerrit Voerman is director of the Documentation Centre Dutch Political Parties, University of Groningen, the Netherlands.
Bd. 13, 2006, 168 S., 19,90 €, br.,
ISBN 3-8258-7668-3

Stephan Bierling; Karlfriedrich Herb; Jerzy Maćków; Martin Sebaldt
Politischen Wandel denken
Herausforderungen der Demokratie in europäischer und globaler Perspektive. Antrittsvorlesung Institut für Politikwissenschaft der Universität Regensburg 26./27. Januar 2004
Dass Wandel mit Fortschritt einhergeht, ist ein moderner Gedanke. Er hat heute seine Selbstverständlichkeit verloren. Den vielfältigen Fragen des politischen Wandels geht die gemeinsame Antrittsvorlesung nach, mit der sich die Professoren des Regensburger Instituts für Politikwissenschaft am 26. und 27. Januar 2004 präsentierten. Politischen Wandel denken. Herausforderungen der Demokratie in europäischer und globaler Perspektive – so lautete die gemeinsame Fragestellung. In ihrer Vielfalt und Eigenheit spannen die Vorträge den Bogen von der Reflexion auf das Verhältnis von Wandel und Fortschritt bis hin zu den Herausforderungen, denen die Demokratie heute begegnet.
Bd. 14, 2004, 72 S., 9,90 €, br.,
ISBN 3-8258-7920-8

Lutz Roemheld (Hg.)
Erinnerung an P.-J. Proudhon
Zur Aktualität seines Denkens für die Zukunft der Sozialdemokratie
P.-J. Proudhon – „nur der Kleinbürger, der beständig zwischen dem Kapital und der Arbeit, zwischen der politischen Ökonomie und dem Kommunismus hin- und hergeworfen wird"? (K. Marx: Elend der Philosophie, 1847). Diese Diskriminierung hat wohl am meisten zur Verdrängung Proudhons aus dem kollektiven Gedächtnis von Sozialisten und Sozialdemokraten beigetragen. Nach dem Scheitern des Sozialismus Marx-Engels'scher Provenienz

LIT Verlag Münster – Berlin – Hamburg – London – Wien
Grevener Str./Fresnostr. 2 48159 Münster
Tel.: 0251 – 62 032 22 – Fax: 0251 – 23 19 72
e-Mail: vertrieb@lit-verlag.de – http://www.lit-verlag.de

kann ein Erinnern an Proudhons libertären Sozialismus Hinweise auf die Möglichkeit der Entwicklung einer „sozialpflichtigen Moderne" (Gerhard Senft) im 21. Jahrhundert geben.
Bd. 15, 2005, 296 S., 24,90 €, br.,
ISBN 3-8258-8292-6

Jürgen H. Wolff
Entwicklungshilfe: Ein hilfreiches Gewerbe?
Versuch einer Bilanz
Die Lebensbedingungen auf der Welt, insbesondere in den Entwick-lungsländern, sollen sich, so hört man es oft, laufend verschlechtern. Insbesondere Institutionen, die von und für die Entwicklungs-hilfe leben, vertreten diese These. Mit reichem Datenmaterial belegt der Verfasser, daß fast überall auf der Welt die Lebenserwartung steigt, sich Bildungsstand und Ernährungslage verbessern, kurz, der Wohlstand zunimmt. Mit einer Ausnahme: Schwarzafrika. Wolff geht weiter, er warnt vor dem Trugschluß, dies sei auf Entwicklungshilfe zurückzuführen und erfolgreiche Entwicklungsprojekte seien mit erfolgreicher Entwicklung gleichzusetzen. Reformvorschläge für die Entwicklungshilfe schließen den Band ab.
Bd. 18, 2005, 320 S., 19,90 €, br.,
ISBN 3-8258-8162-8

Wolfgang Gieler (Hg.)
Internationale Wirtschaftsorganisationen
Entstehung – Struktur – Perspektiven. Ein Handbuch
Das „Handbuch Internationale Wirtschaftsorganisationen" informiert über die Außenwirtschaftspolitiken internationaler Organisationen. Zur besseren Handhabbarkeit verfügen die einzelnen Beiträge über einen vergleichbaren Aufbau – Gründungsgeschichte und Gründungsmotivation, vertragliche Grundlage und Struktur, integrationstheoretische Einordnung und Perspektiven sowie eine Auswahlbibliographie. Der Band wendet sich an einen breiten Benutzerkreis in Forschung und Lehre, in Politik, Verwaltung und Medien sowie an alle politisch Interessierten.
Bd. 19, 2005, 416 S., 24,90 €, br.,
ISBN 3-8258-8532-1

Christiane Lemke
Amerika-Bilder: US-Politik zwischen Moralisierung und Macht
Die transatlantischen Beziehungen zeichnen sich durch widersprüchliche Deutungsmuster aus. Einerseits gilt die US-amerikanische Gesellschaft als weltoffen und innovationsfreudig, andererseits erscheint sie aber auch als konservativ und traditionell. Die Spannungen zwischen Tradition und Moderne speisen das ambivalente Bild von „zwei Amerikas", welches den Blick von Europa auf die Vereinigten Staaten prägt. Basierend auf langjährigen Forschungsarbeiten und eingehenden Kenntnissen gesellschaftlicher und politischer Entwicklungen in den Vereinigten Staaten analysiert die Verfasserin, ausgehend von den Präsidentschaftswahlen 2004, längerfristige Veränderungen in der amerikanischen Politik. Sie zeigt die Widersprüche und Ungleichzeitigkeiten auf, die die amerikanische Politik in einer Zeit kennzeichnen, welche durch einen wachsenden Einfluss von moralischen Werte- und Orientierungsmustern in der Politik charakterisiert ist.
Bd. 21, 2005, 128 S., 14,90 €, br.,
ISBN 3-8258-8701-4

Reidar Visser
Basra, the Failed Gulf State
Separatism and Nationalism in Southern Iraq
Is Iraq "artificial", on the verge of disintegrating? All too often, the answers to this question ignore Iraq's own history. In fact, the literature on indigenous attempts at dismembering Iraq is surprisingly patchy, especially with regard to the oil-rich south. This book presents, for the first time, an actual case of southern Iraqi separatism: a daring bid to turn Basra into a pro-British mercantile mini-state. The study uncovers the dynamics and limits of southern separatism, casts new light on the victory of Iraqi nationalism in the south

and discusses the challenges of post-2003 regionalism in a federal Iraq. *"From the abundance of recent publications on modern Iraq, Reidar Visser's work on the origins and development of twentieth-century separatism in the southern region of that country stands out. For anyone seriously interested in the current conflict in Iraq over the question of federalism versus centralism, this meticulously researched study provides a highly instructive historical perspective."* –Werner Ende, professor emeritus of Islamic Studies at Albert-Ludwigs-Universität, Freiburg, Germany
Bd. 22, 2005, 256 S., 29,90 €, br.,
ISBN 3-8258-8799-5

Barbara Wasner
Alterssicherung in Europa: Institutionenwandel durch Europäisierung?
Europäisierung wird in der öffentlichen Diskussion häufig mit der „Fremdbestimmung aus Brüssel" gleichgesetzt. Und auch im sozialwissenschaftlichen Diskurs bleibt der Begriff unbestimmt und wenig eindeutig. In diesem Buch werden die verschiedenen Begriffsbedeutungen geordnet, zueinander in Beziehung gesetzt und so zu einem theoretischen Konzept ausgearbeitet, das auf die Wandlungen der Alterssicherungssysteme konzeptionell angewandt werden kann. Das Buch stellt eine umfassende Analyse der verschiedenen Alterssicherungssysteme der Mitgliedstaaten der EU und ihre Reaktionen auf die europäische „Herausforderung" dar.
Bd. 23, 2005, 376 S., 24,90 €, br.,
ISBN 3-8258-8855-x

Mario Petri; Ulrich Schnier; Jürgen Bellers (Hg.)
Handbuch der transitorischen Systeme, Diktaturen und autoritären Regime der Gegenwart
Gefestigte und intakte sowie gesellschaftlich akzeptierte und vor allem „funktionierende", demokratische Strukturen sind heutzutage keine Selbstverständlichkeit, schon gar nicht in globaler Perspektive. Auf dem steinigen Weg zu demokratischen Strukturen liefert das Handbuch der transitorischen Systeme, Diktaturen und autoritären Regime eine Bestandsaufnahme anhand einer Vielzahl ausgesuchter nationalstaatlicher Beispiele. Die strukturell ähnlich angelegten Beiträge skizzieren neben der Historie das gegenwärtige politische System und liefern einen Ausblick zu Chancen und Perspektiven des weiteren Demokratisierungsprozesses. Ergänzt werden die aktuellen Nationalstaatsbeispiele um Betrachtungen der „klassischen" totalitären, diktatorischen und autoritären Regime des deutschen Nationalsozialismus, des italienischen Faschismus, des spanischen Franquismus sowie des Austro-Faschismus.
Bd. 24, 2006, 584 S., 39,90 €, br.,
ISBN 3-8258-9070-8

Hartmut Elsenhans
Globalization Between A Convoy Model and An Underconsumptionist Threat
There are different types of globalization. Today's globalization is characterized by the worldwide disempowerment of labor. This is the result not of low real wages in backward countries but of devaluation-driven exports from relatively prosperous catch-up countries. An alternative form of globalization, the convoy model, is possible if the causes of devaluation-driven exports are eliminated. This does not call for a worldwide alignment of labor costs, but worldwide full employment policies. The latter require a strong state in labor-surplus economies of the underdeveloped South in addition to social and economic reforms in favor of the poor.
Bd. 25, 2006, 312 S., 29,90 €, br.,
ISBN 3-8258-9219-0

LIT Verlag Münster – Berlin – Hamburg – London – Wien
Grevener Str./Fresnostr. 2 48159 Münster
Tel.: 0251 – 62 032 22 – Fax: 0251 – 23 19 72
e-Mail: vertrieb@lit-verlag.de – http://www.lit-verlag.de